CD

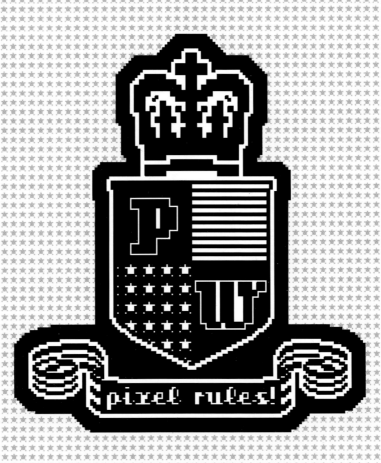

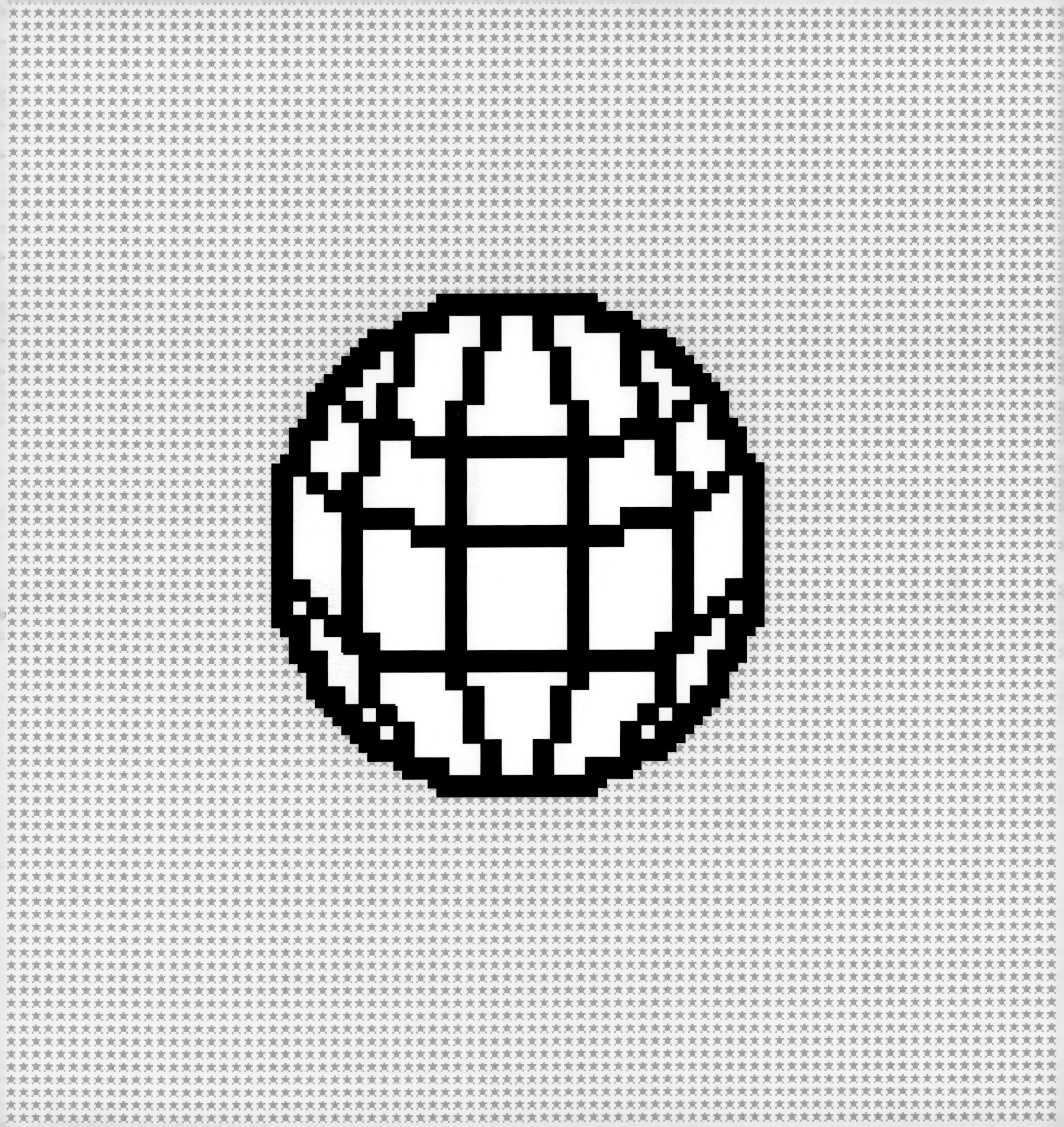

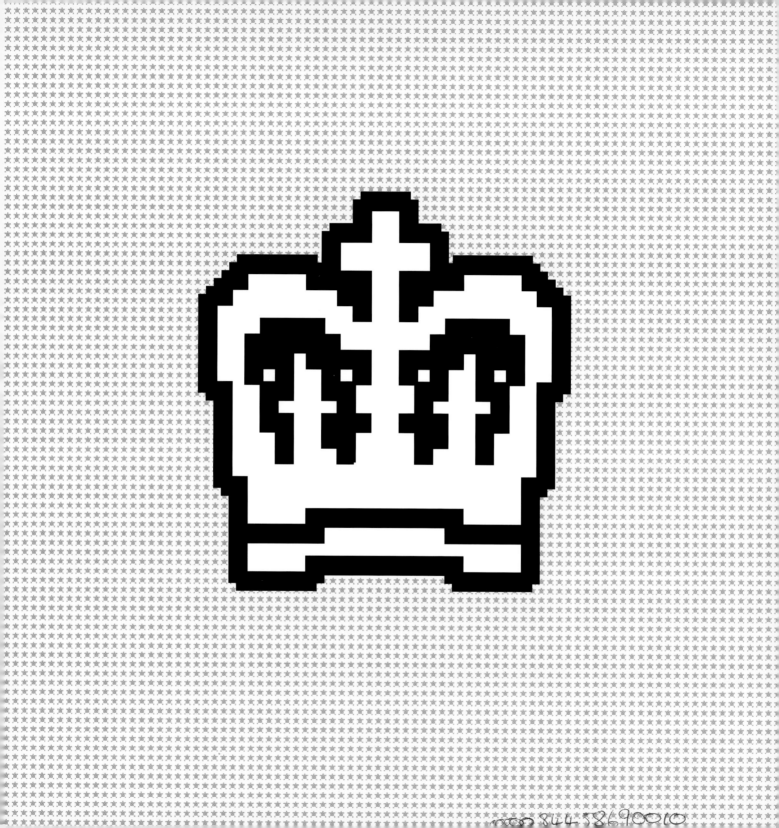

pixelworld

A pixel is defined as one screen point on a common type of graphics monitor, which employs a raster-scan display. It is the smallest unit of an image produced on a computer screen. Back in the days of Apple II or 8086 home-computing, monitors could show only a limited number of colours and pixels. Requiring a higher processing speed, anti-aliasing algorithms were seldom applied. So pixel graphics became the standard in for most home-computing interfaces and video games.

As the Internet has entered our lives, many web designers turned their visions to pixel graphics due to their fast-loading performance for overcoming bandwidth and web-browser problems. Many pixel pushers also used web as a platform to announce their works to the world. These factors served to catalyze the development of pixel graphics.

One of the greatest attractions of pixel graphics is the amazingly detailed composition they allow. No matter whether it's a huge canvas of a pixel city or a sophisticated, built-engine interface, the degree of detail is explicitly illustrated. On the other hand, a basic constraint of pixel graphics are their limited colour palette. However, this deficiency has created a unique style in itself, an aesthetics of crispness and squares.

Today's pixel graphic not only caters for low-resolution desktop icons and low-bandwidth Internet connections. It has become a new form of art. It is often used to illustrate clean, playful and impres-sive images, as well as giving a certain kind of minimalistic expression. Pixel graphics have featured in different digital media including web, graphics and broadcast. They are no longer framed inside digital boundaries and

will extend to tangible media with a three-dimensional form in the near future.

Pixel World comprises the pixel works of 31 entities from all over the world. These have been catego-rized into four groups: Pixel City, Pixel People, Pixel Things and Pixel Art, which will reveal some of the most significant possibilities of this spectacular graphic medium.

We trust these examples will both delight and inspire you. If it's something you've never really considered before, perhaps now is the time to start becoming "pixelated"!

contributors

200ok *Berlin*   Adept Vormgeving *Amsterdam*
Ala Webstatt *Switerland*   Arjan Westerdiep
Eindhoven   Brian Taylor *Scotland*   Craig Kroeger
Wisconsin   Delaware *Japan*   Dong Jianwei *China*
Eboy *Berlin*   Francis Lam *Hong Kong*   Hideaki Ohtani
Japan   Ian Warner *Berlin*   Isao Yamanaka *Japan*
Itai Rabinowitz *Israel*   Jonas Loefgren *Sweden*
Kim *Malaysia*   Little Factory *Hong Kong*   Lobo
Brazil   Lovepixel *Taiwan*   Masatake Matoba *Japan*
Meomi San Francisco   Quickhoney *New York*   Shinya
Inamura *Japan*   Steffen Schaefer *Germany*   Sulake
Labs *Finland*   Ten_do *Japan*   Tgb Design *Japan*
Toshiyuki Iwasaki *Japan*   Tsuyoshi Kusano *Japan*
Wig_01 *United Kingdom*   Yuji Oshimoto *Japan*

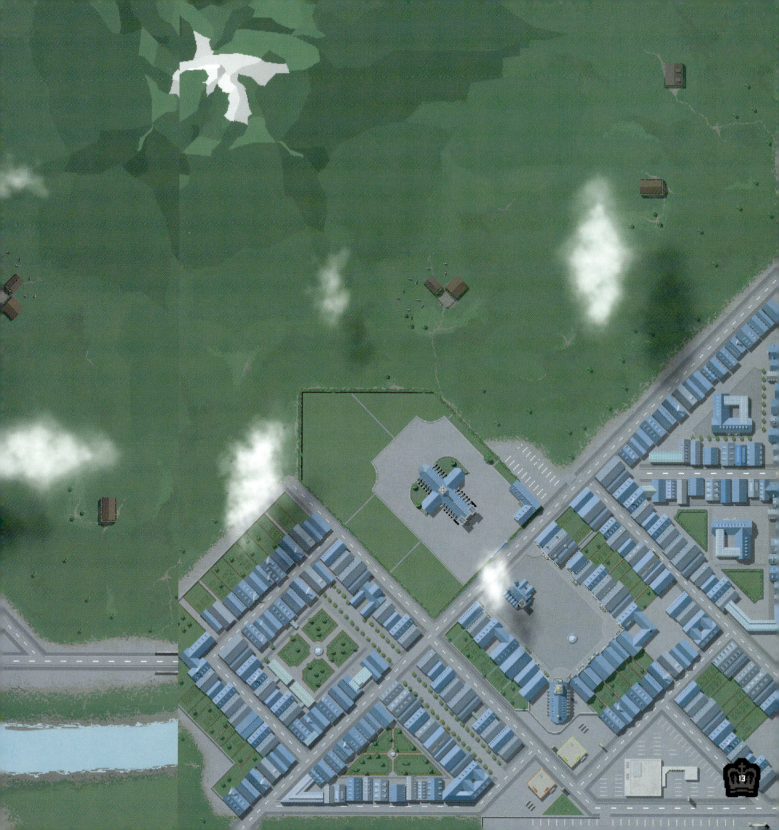

© TOTTO RENNA

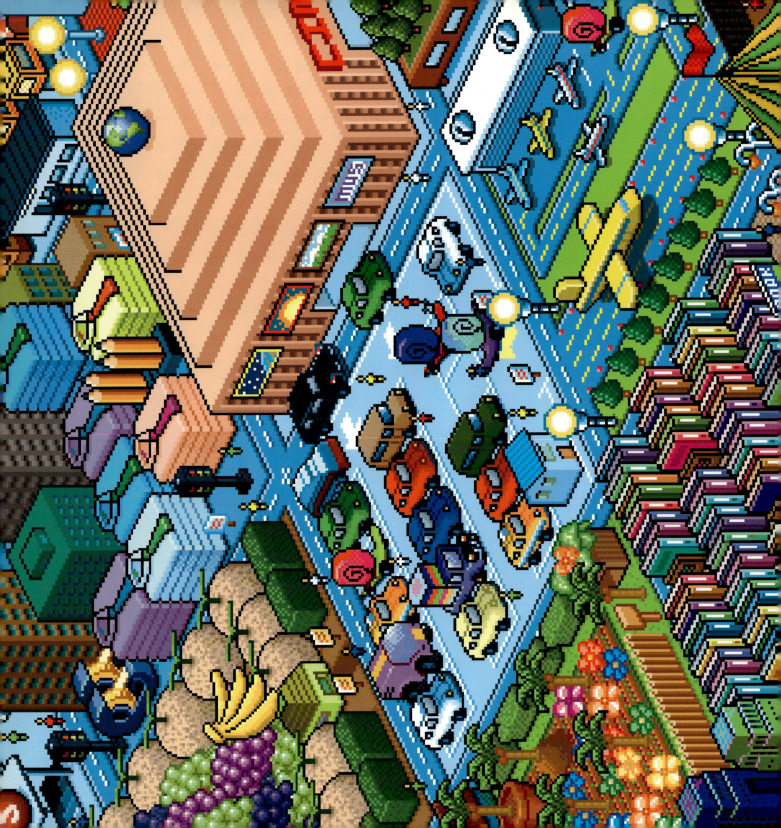

RESTAURANT

29

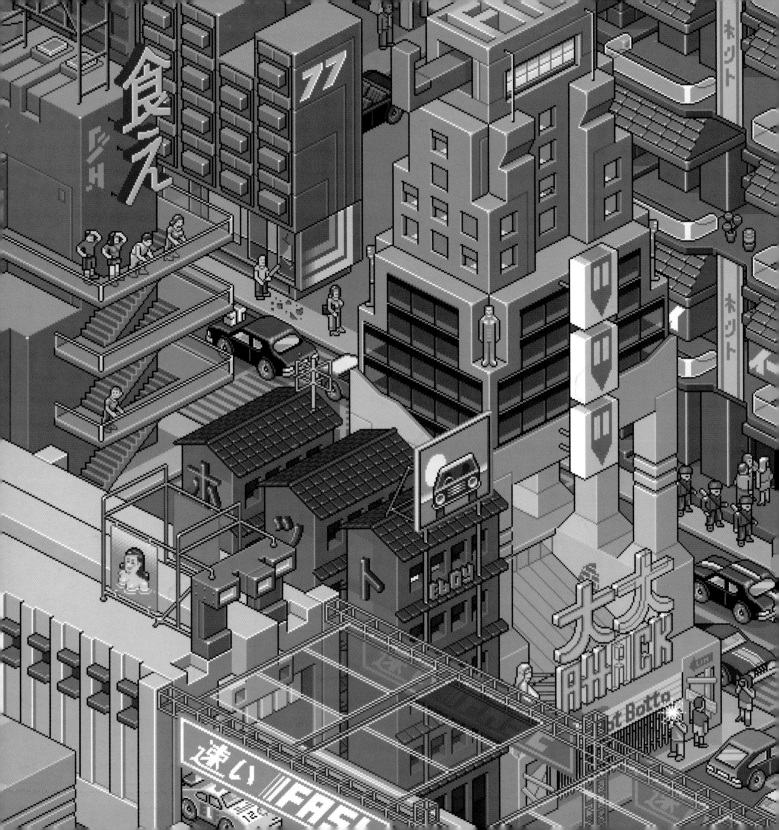

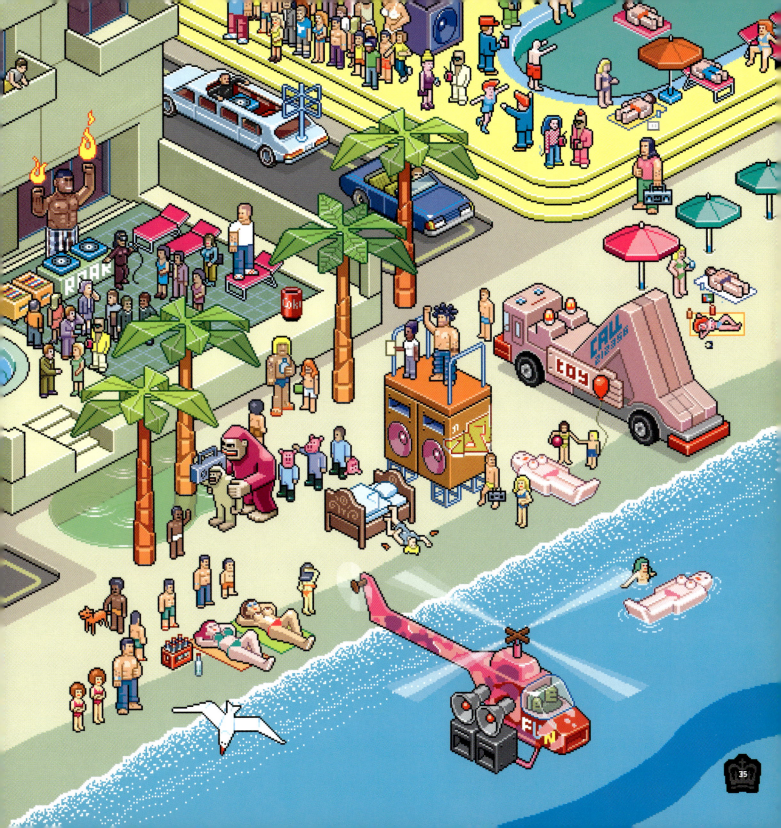

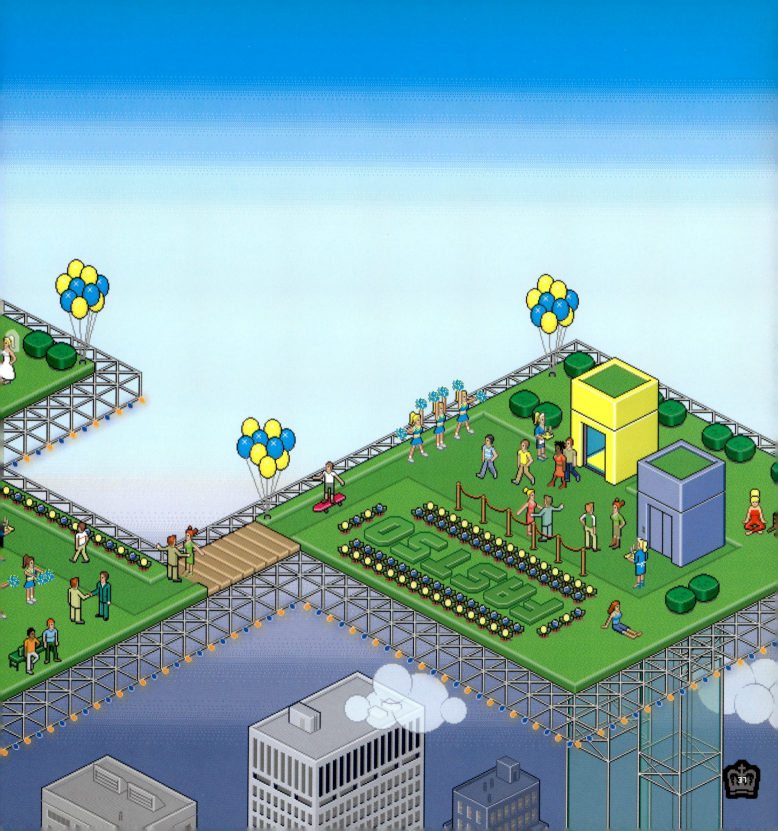

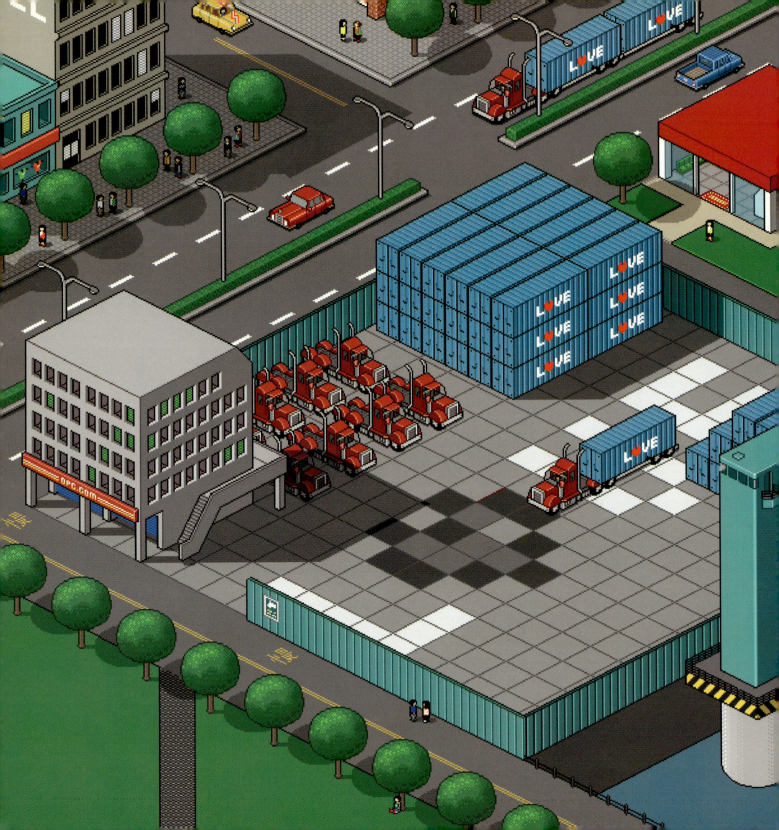

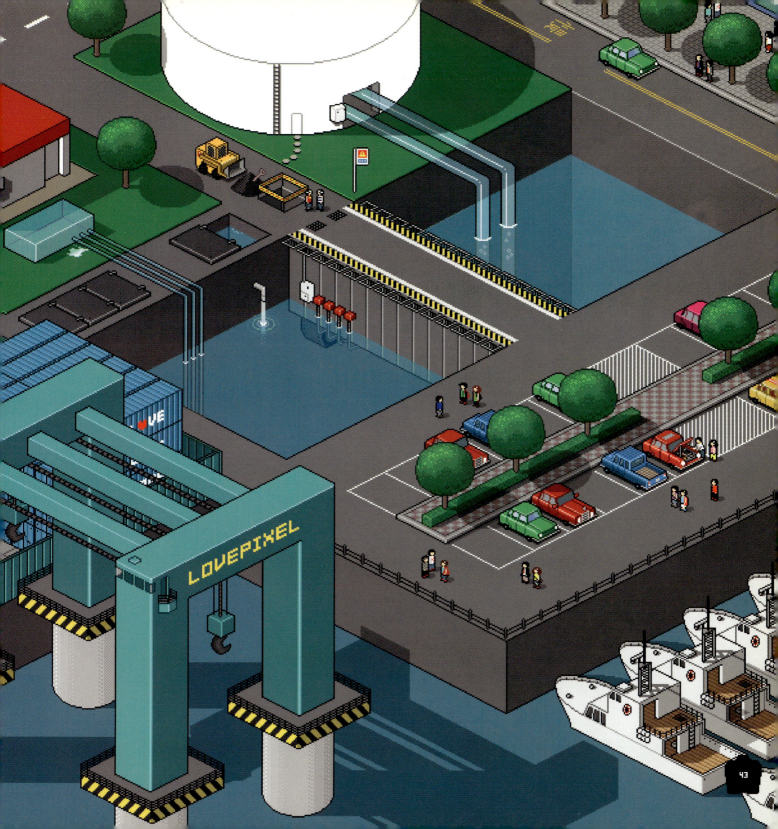

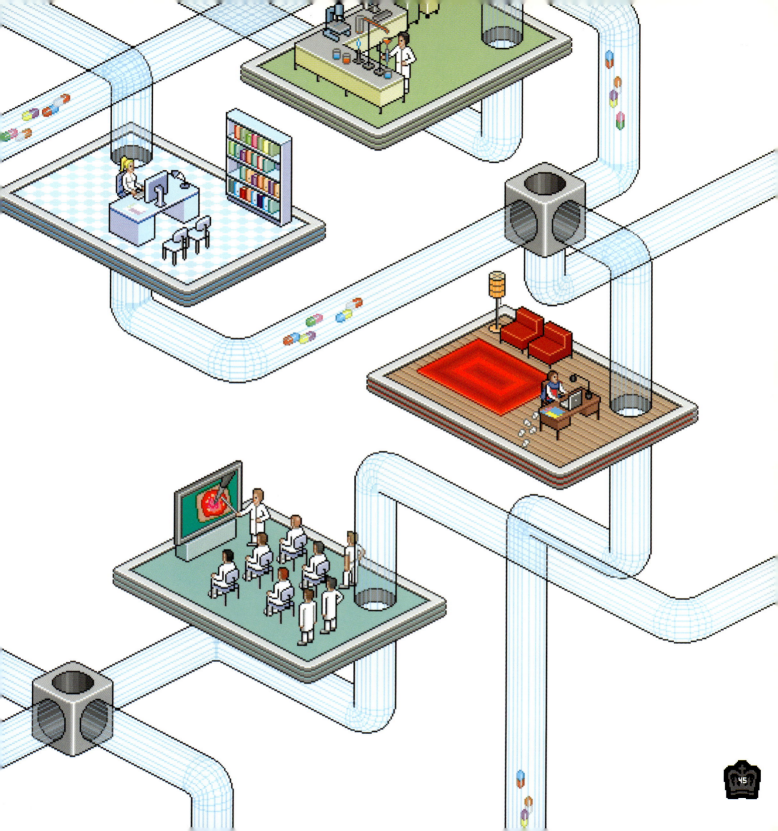

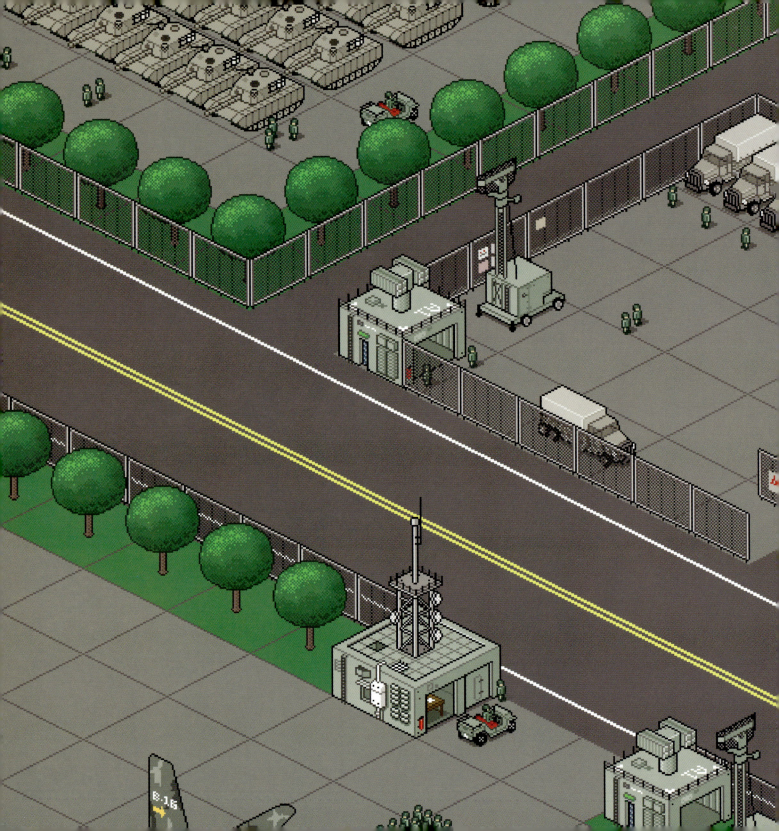

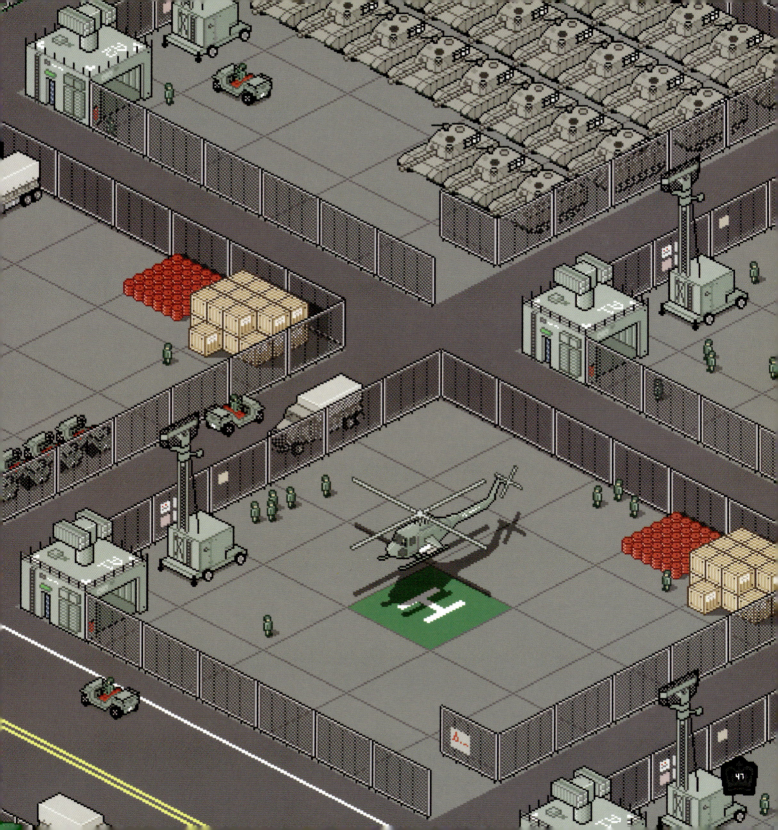

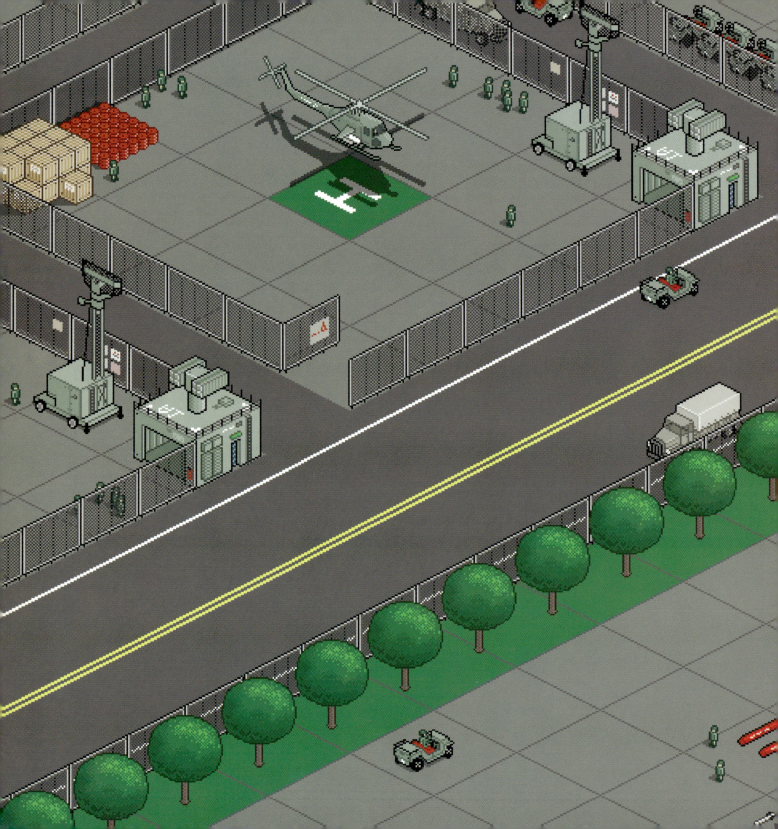

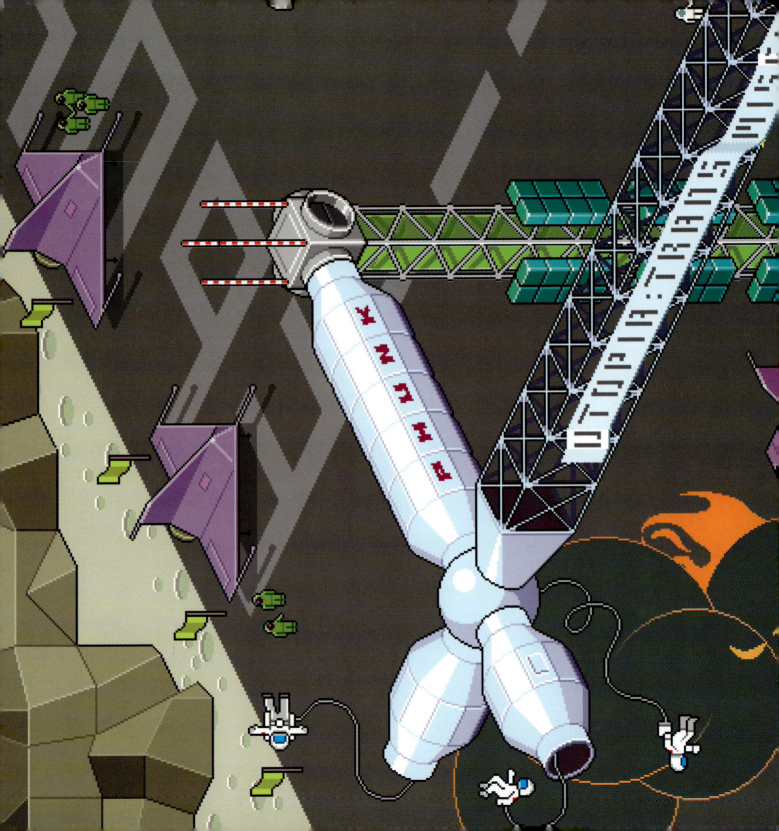

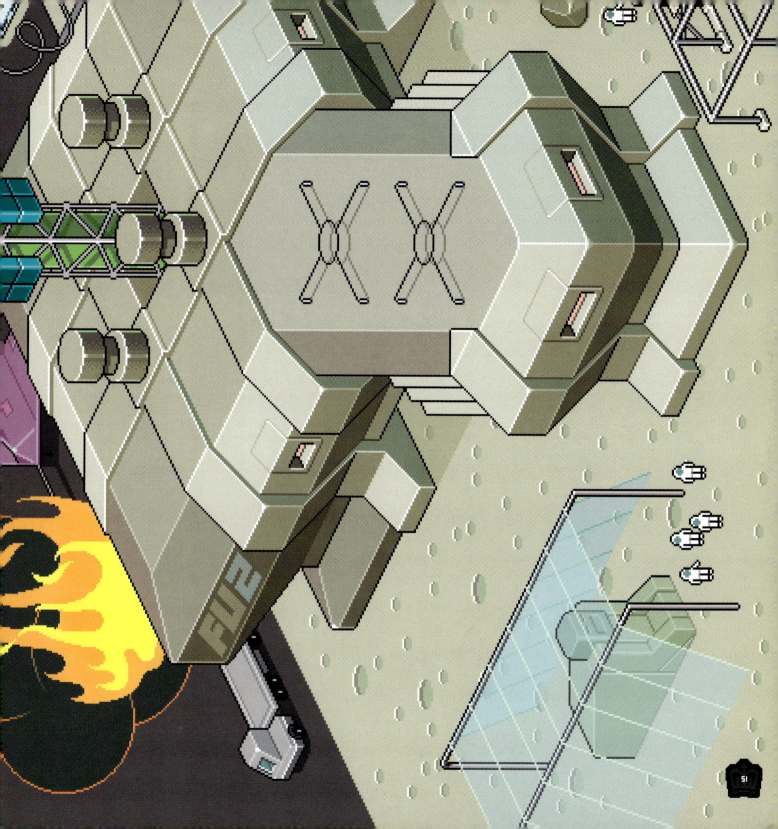

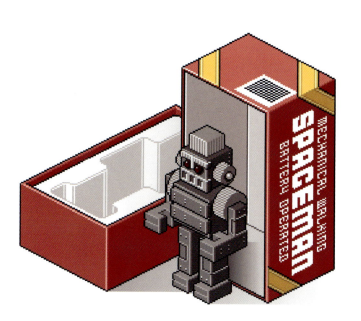

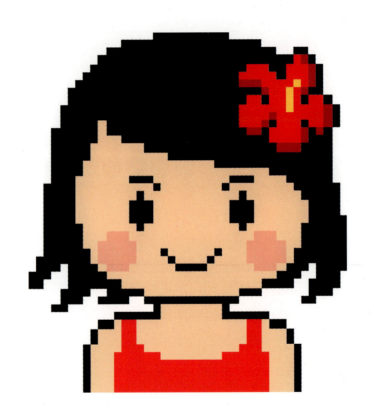

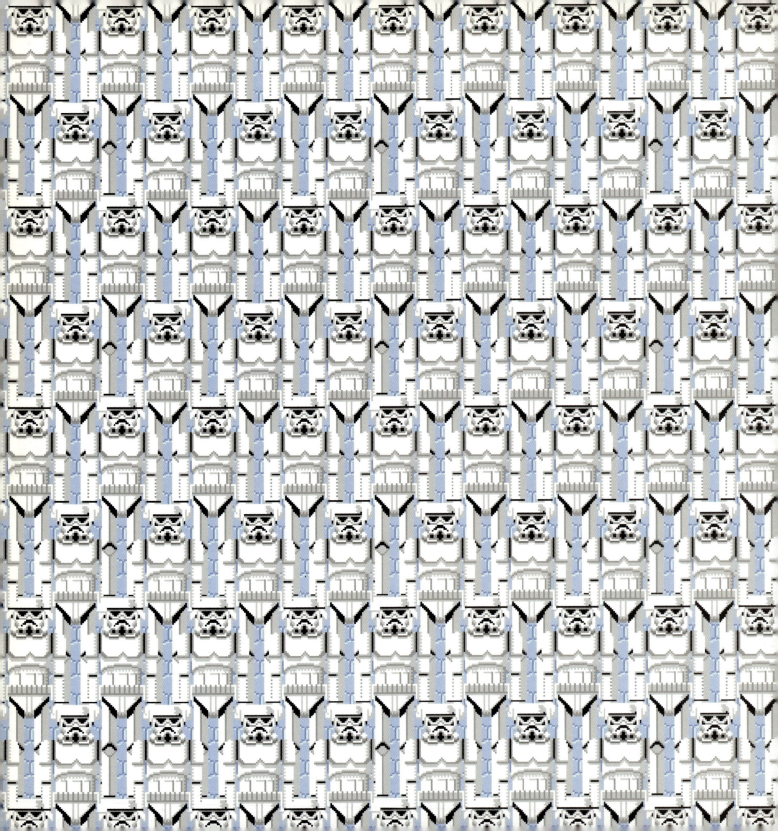

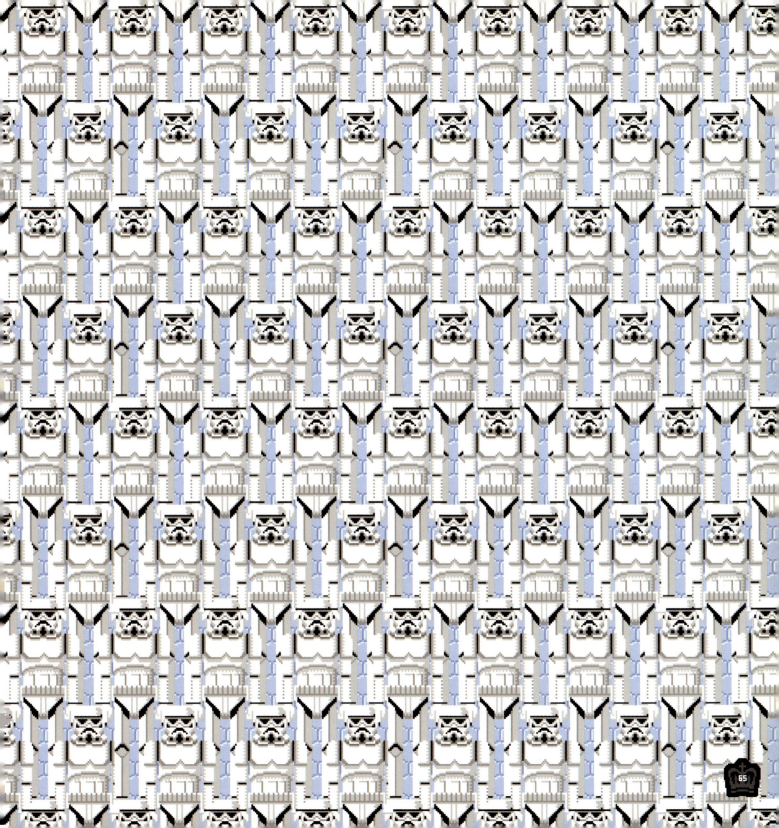

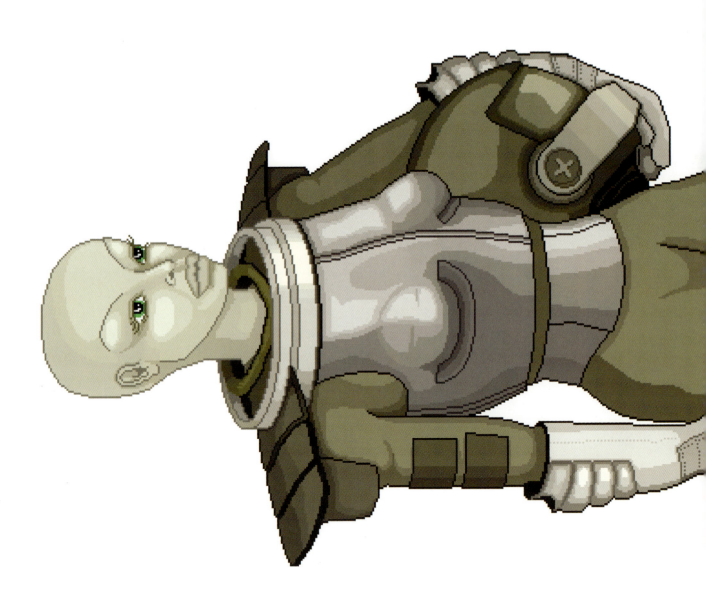

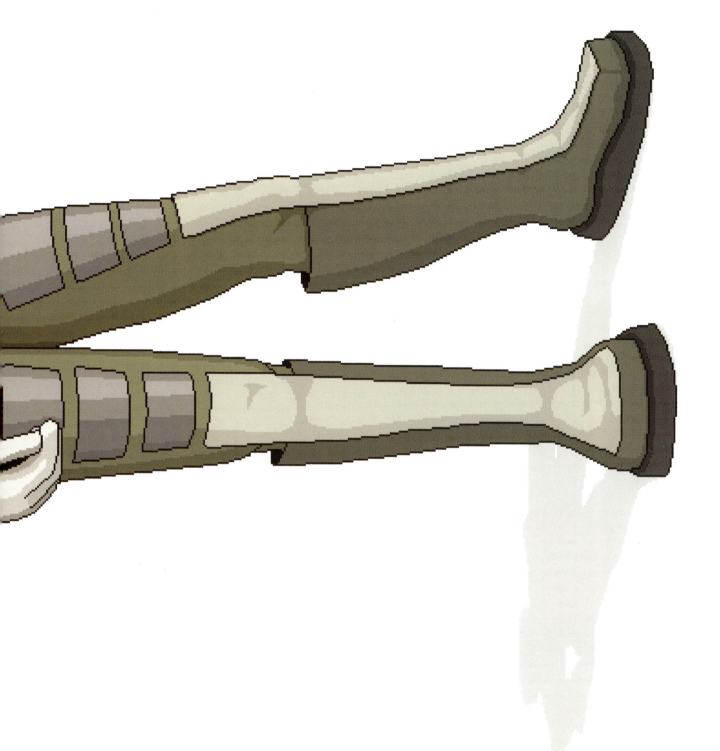

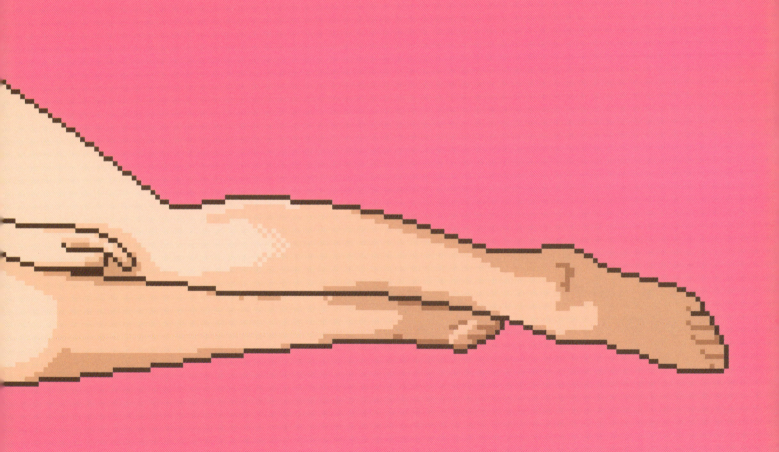

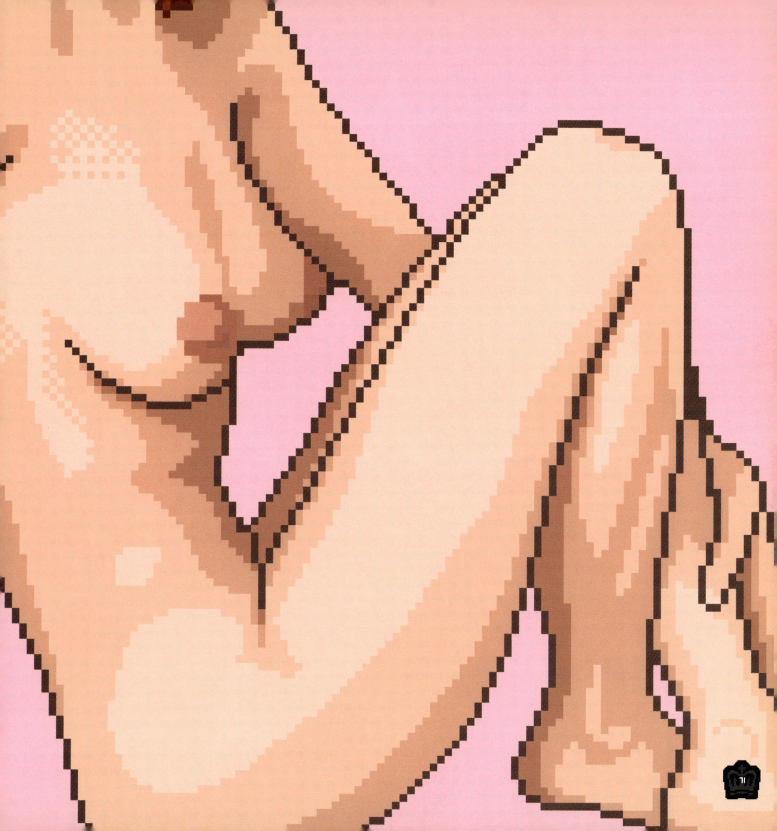

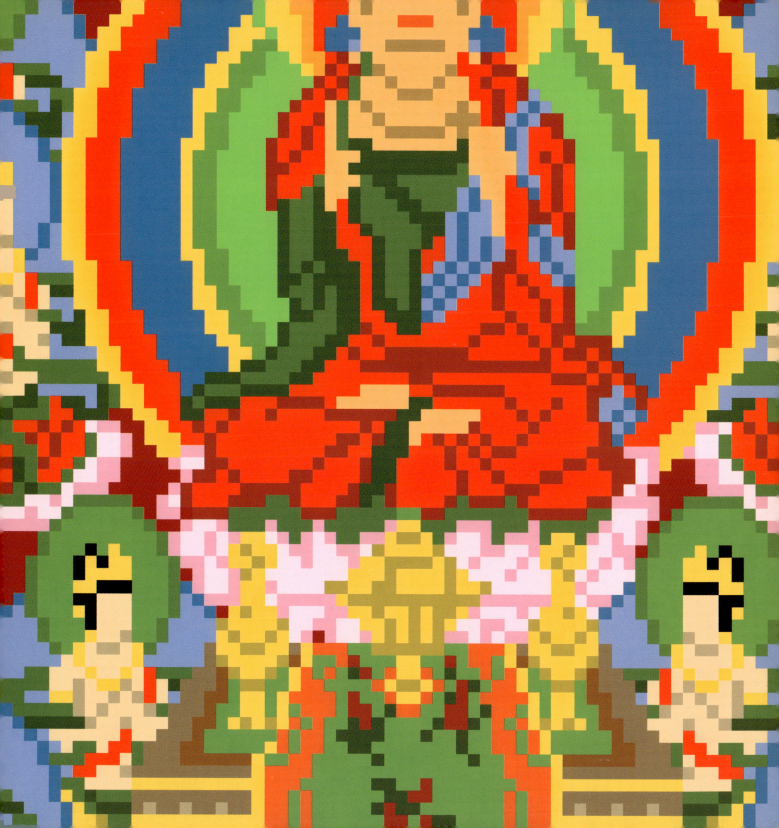

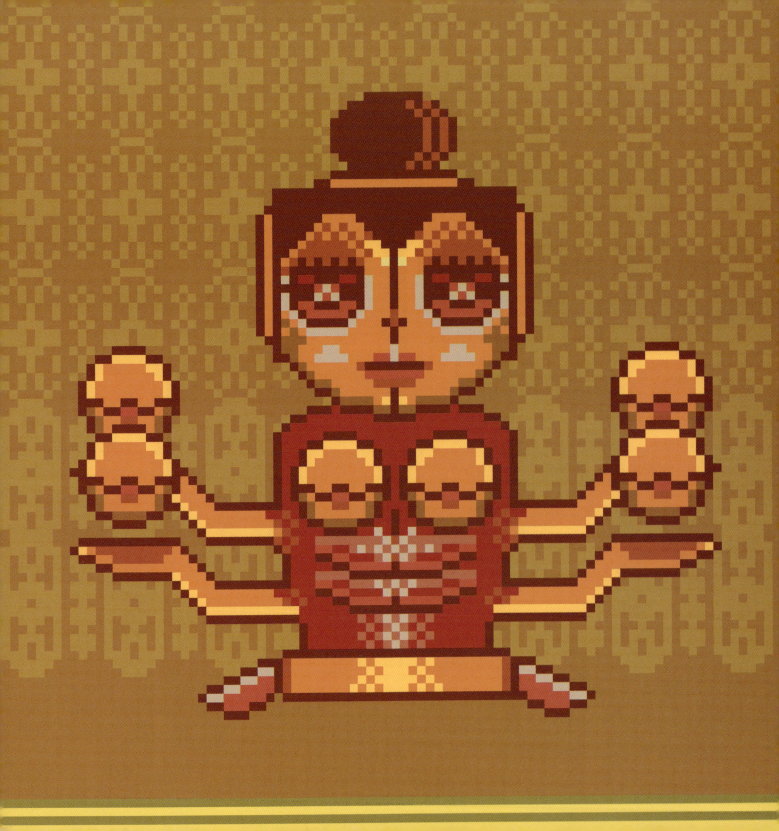

❖❖ Jezie's Traveling Side Show ❖❖

act one : three geisha

act two : dancing bear

act three : sausage dogs

act four : snake lady

act five : juggling shiva

act six : isis triplets

© meomi design 2002

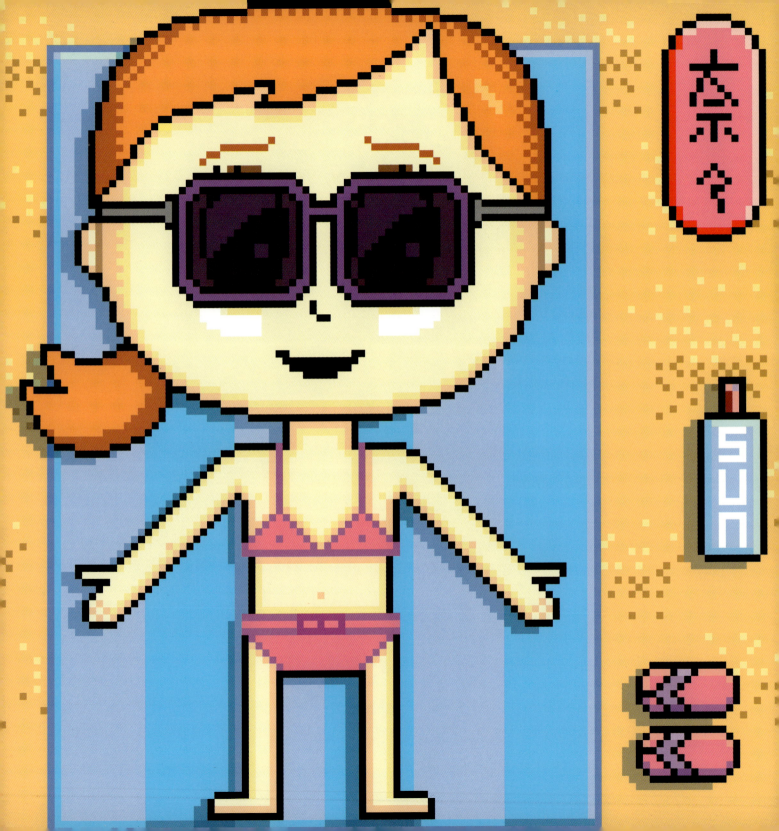

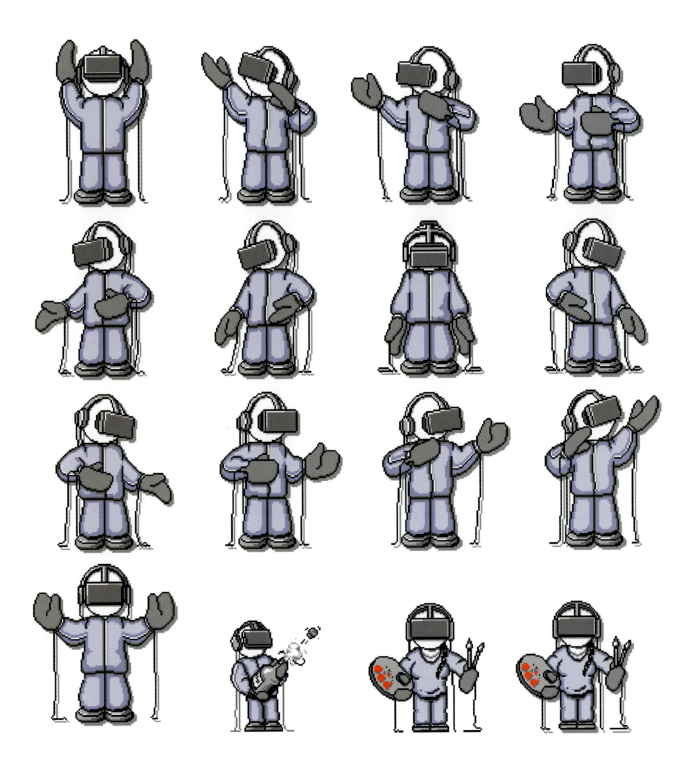

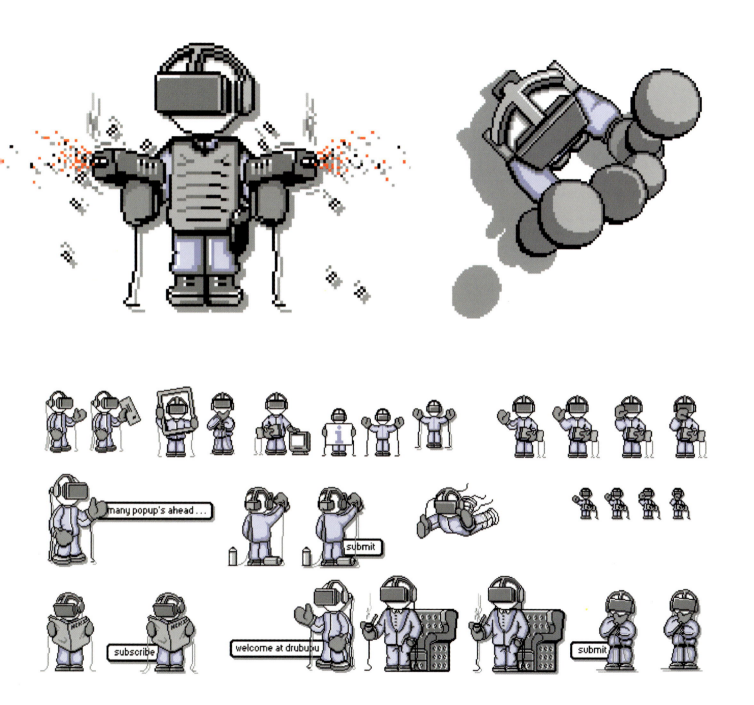

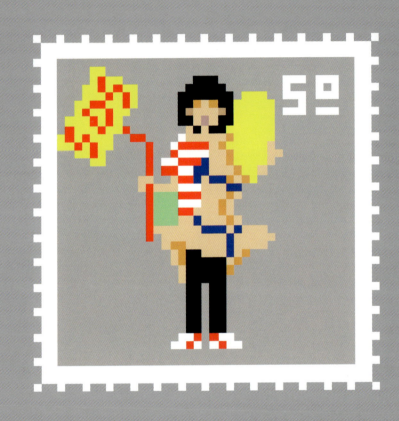

george w.

saddam

tony

osama

jacques

gerhard

ariel

yasser

vladimir

silvio

fidel

muammar

kofi

karol

99

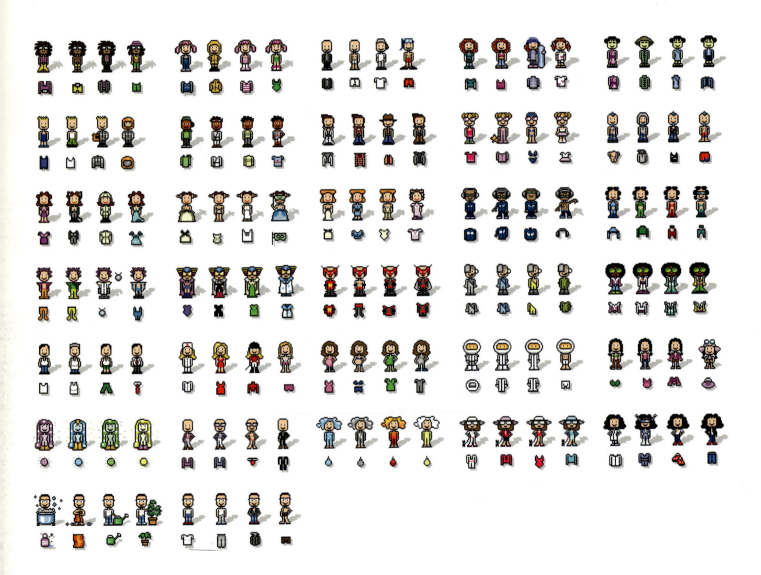

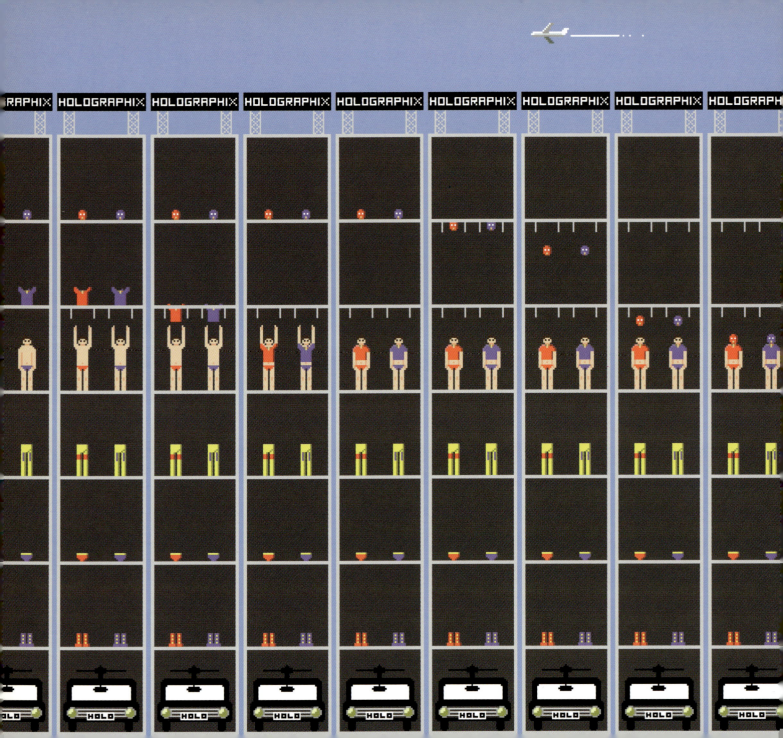

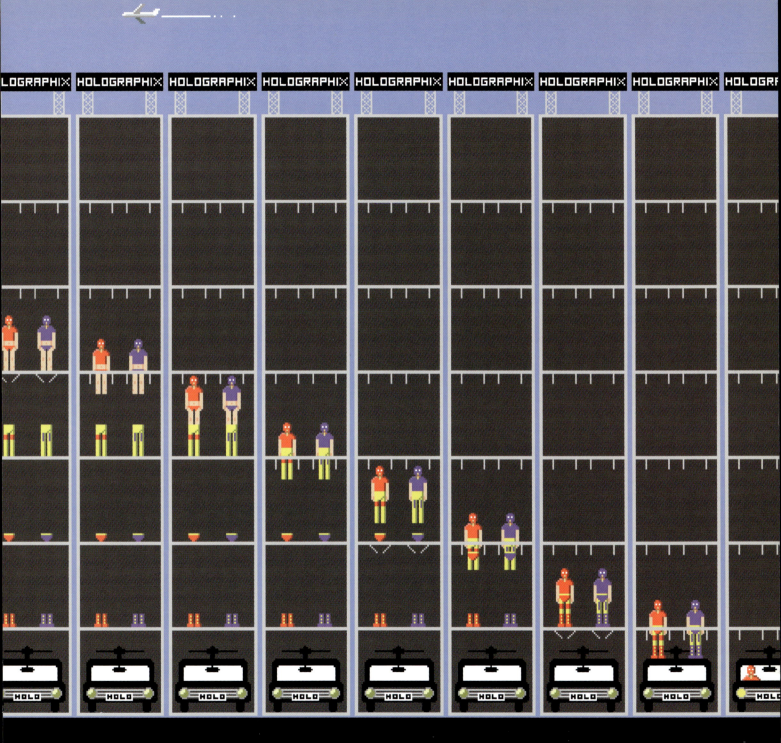

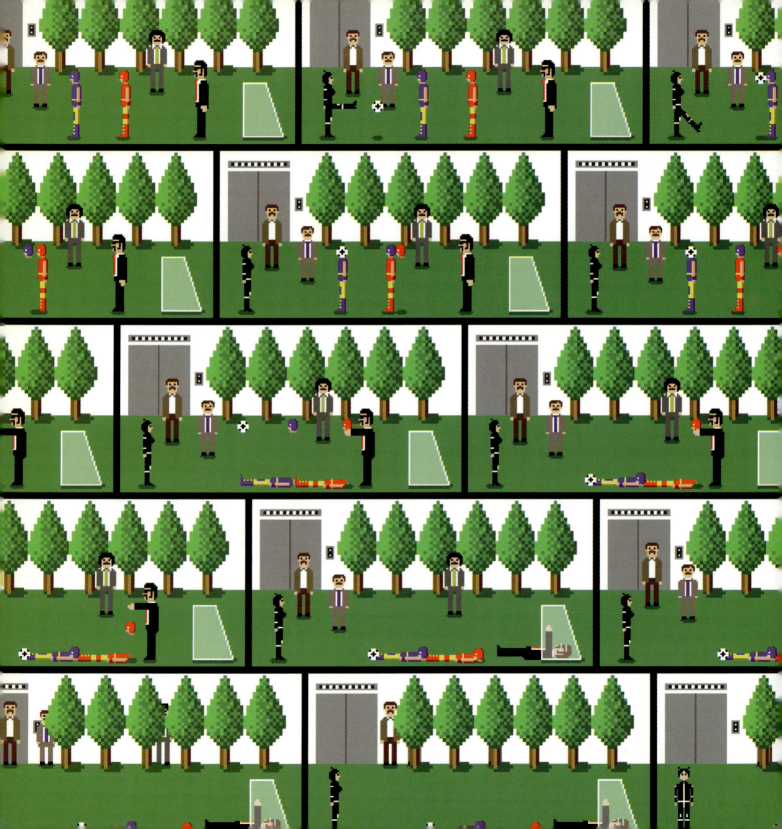

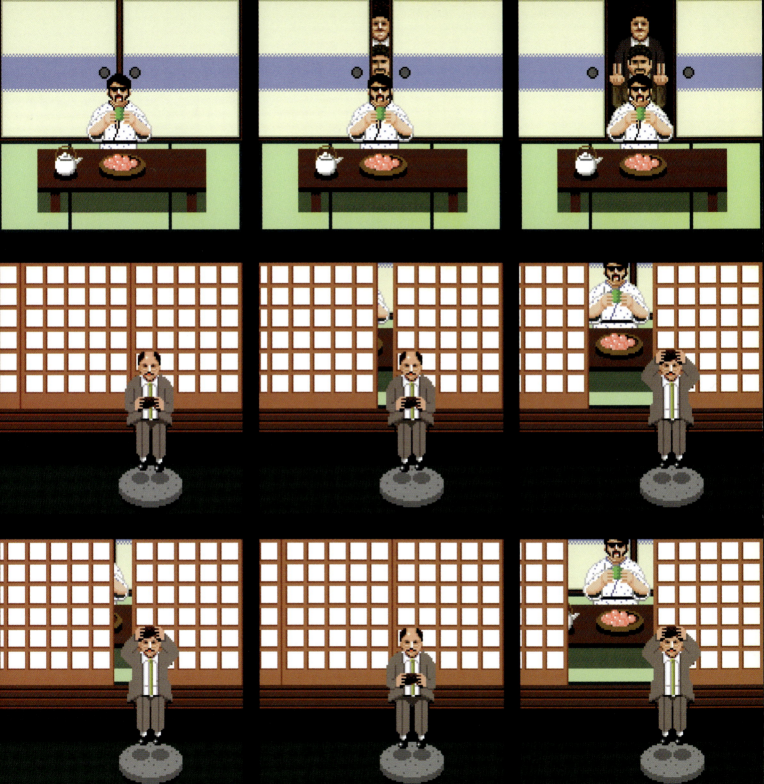

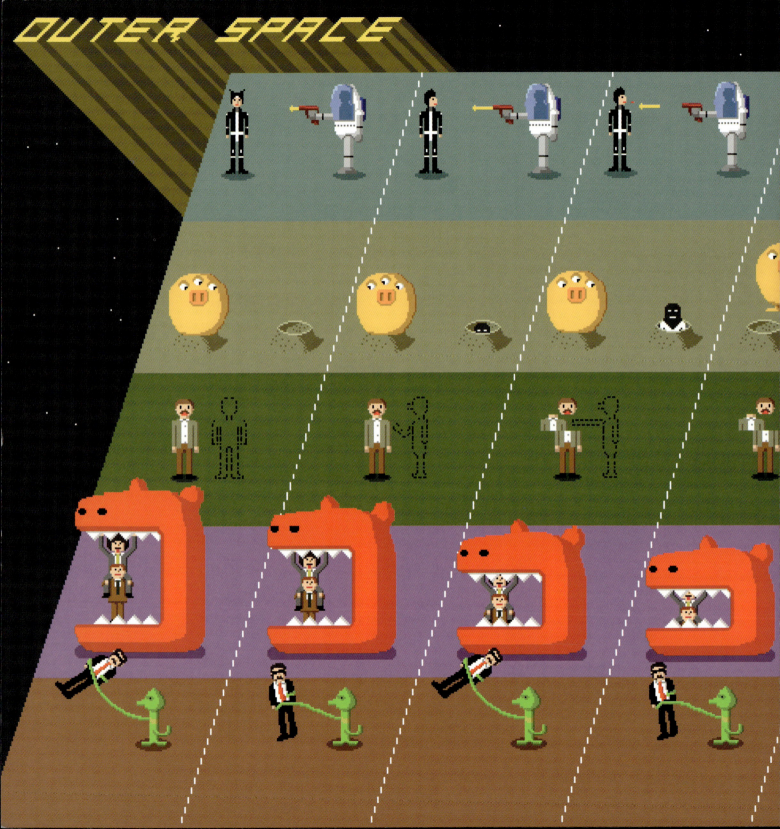

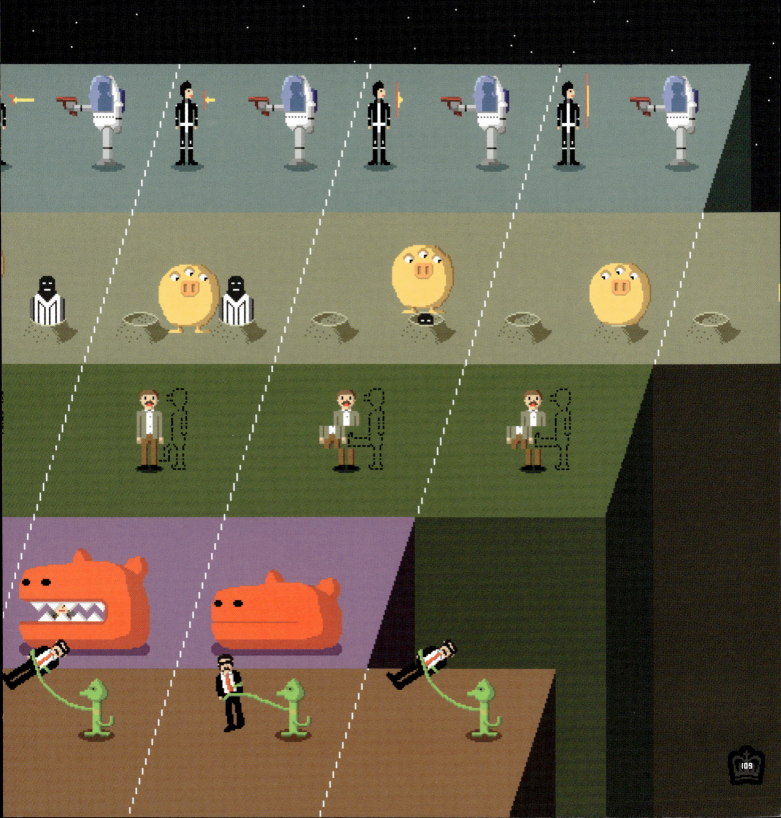

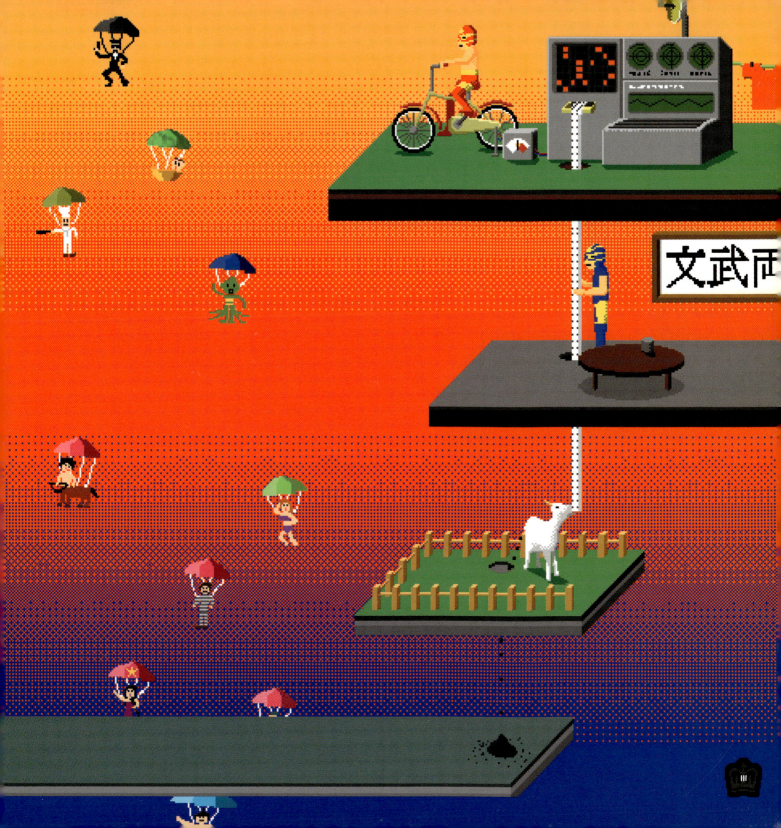

←ELEVATOR
REST ROOM→
PLAYGROUND→
RESTAURANT→

HOLOGRAPHIX

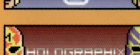
HOLOGRAPHIX

HOLOGRAPHIX

HOLOGRAPHIX

MAIL

URL

HG HG

HOLOGRAPHIX

PARTY HARD

HOLOGRAPHIX

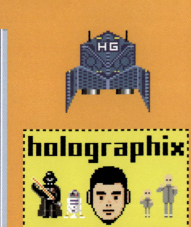
holographix

HG

PLAYHORSE
2002
女性にモテるデザインを!!

WOMAN JOURNAL
YES! COOKING
FASHION
ASTROLOG 100% 当る 占い

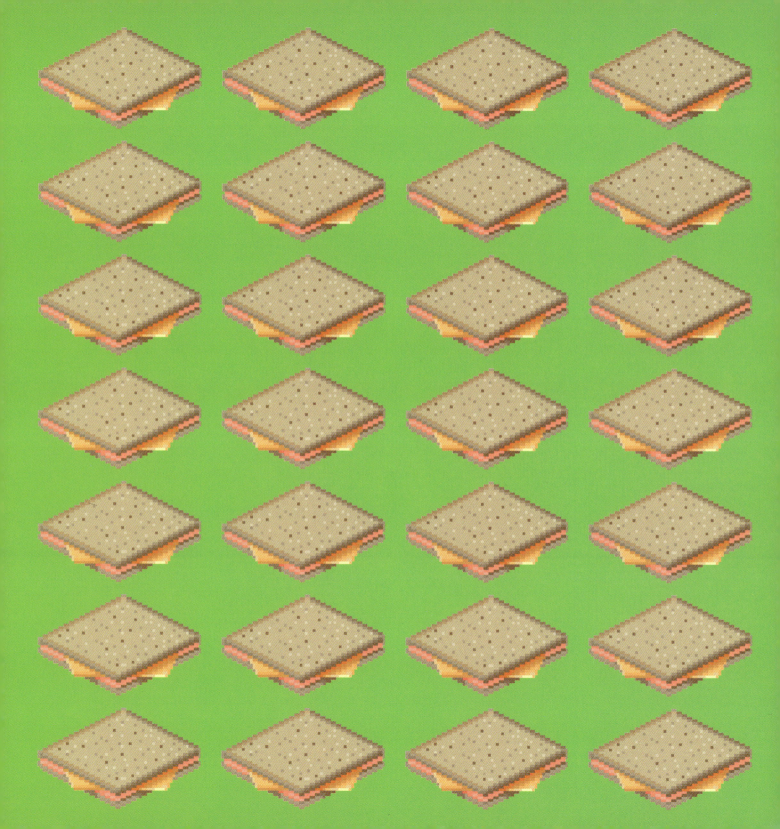

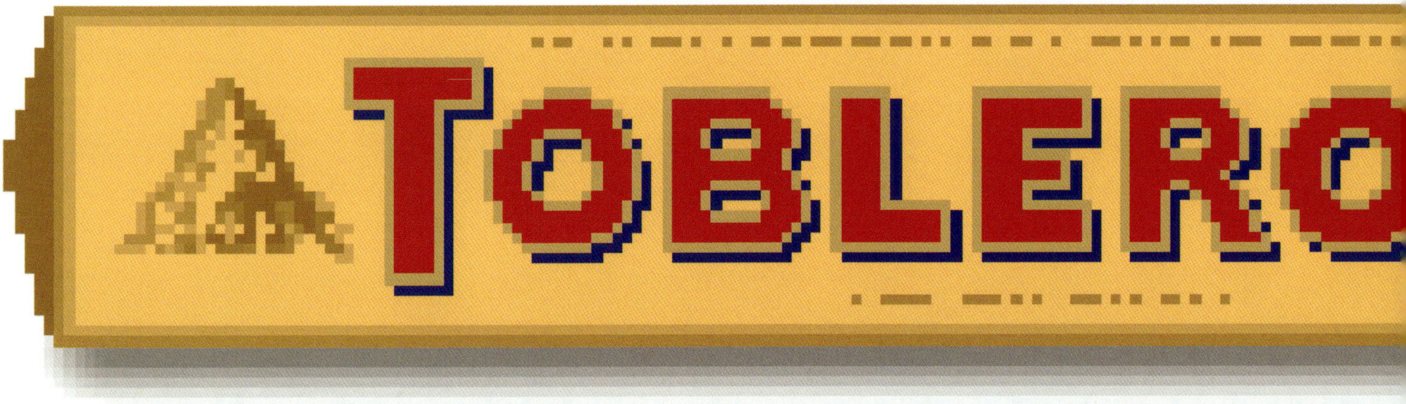
TOBLERO

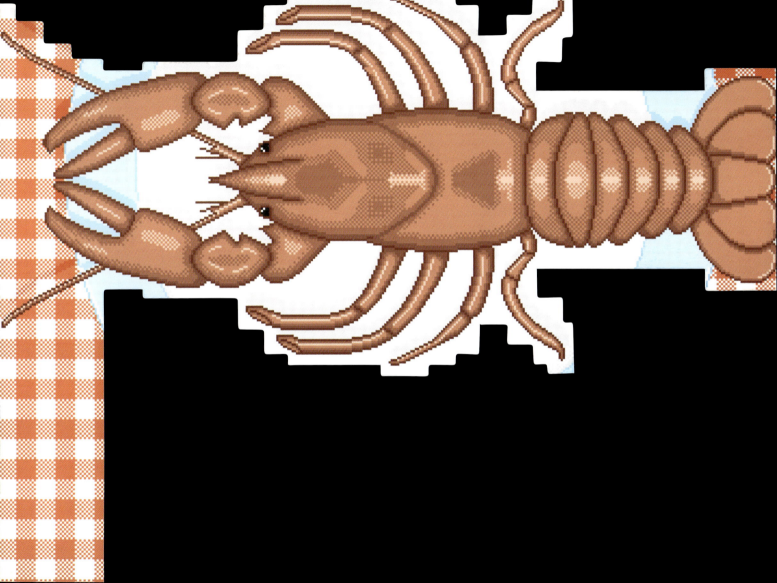

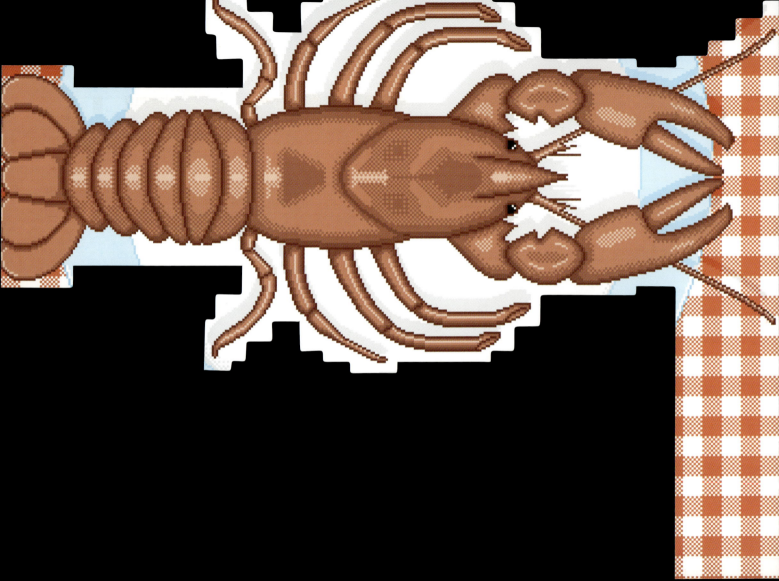

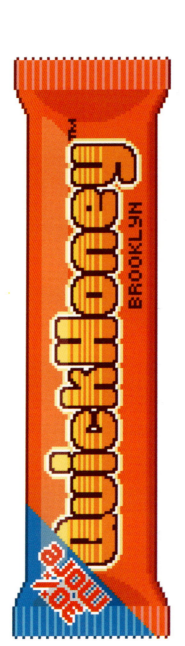

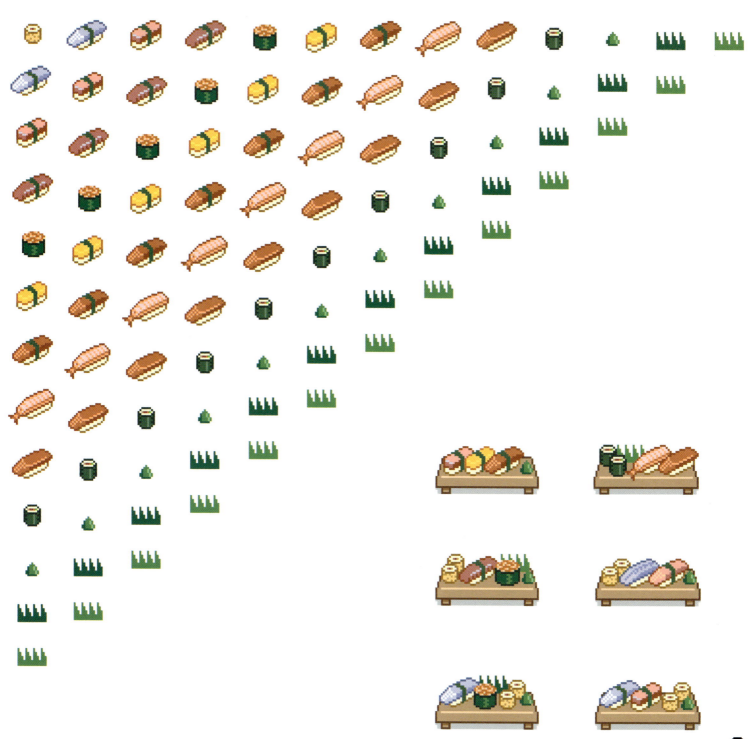

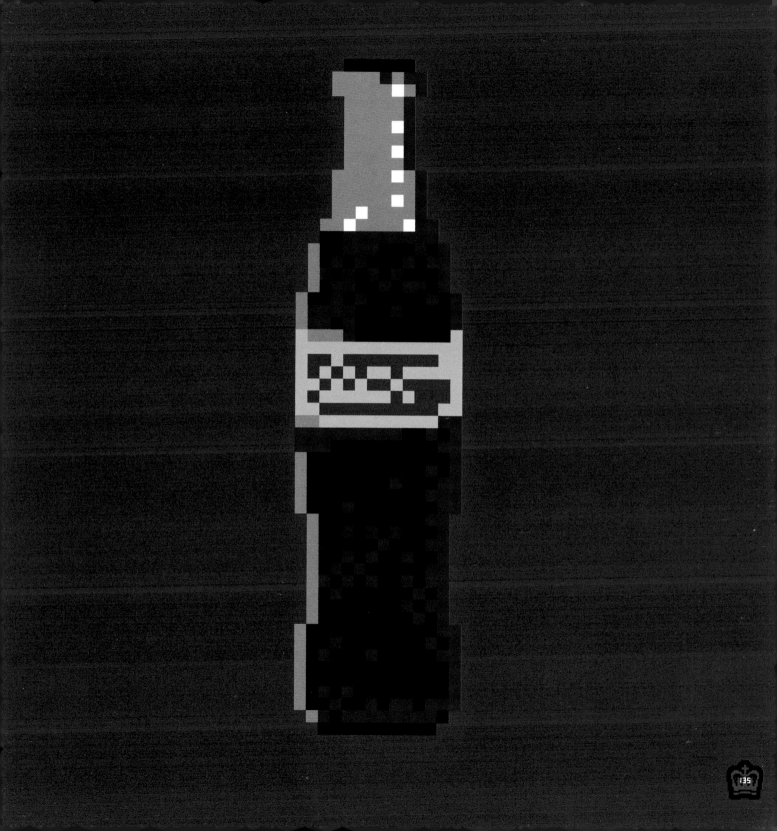

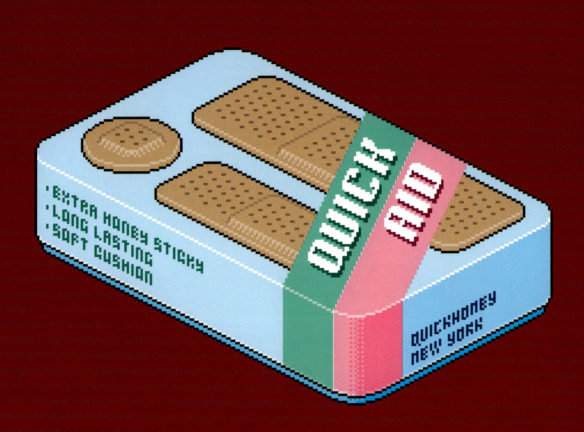

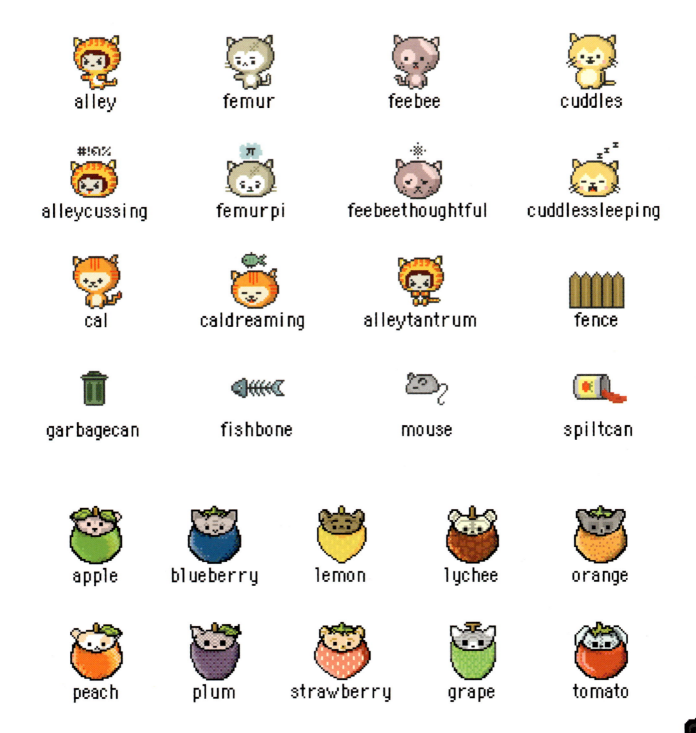

alley

femur

feebee

cuddles

alleycussing

femurpi

feebeethoughtful

cuddlessleeping

cal

caldreaming

alleytantrum

fence

garbagecan

fishbone

mouse

spiltcan

apple

blueberry

lemon

lychee

orange

peach

plum

strawberry

grape

tomato

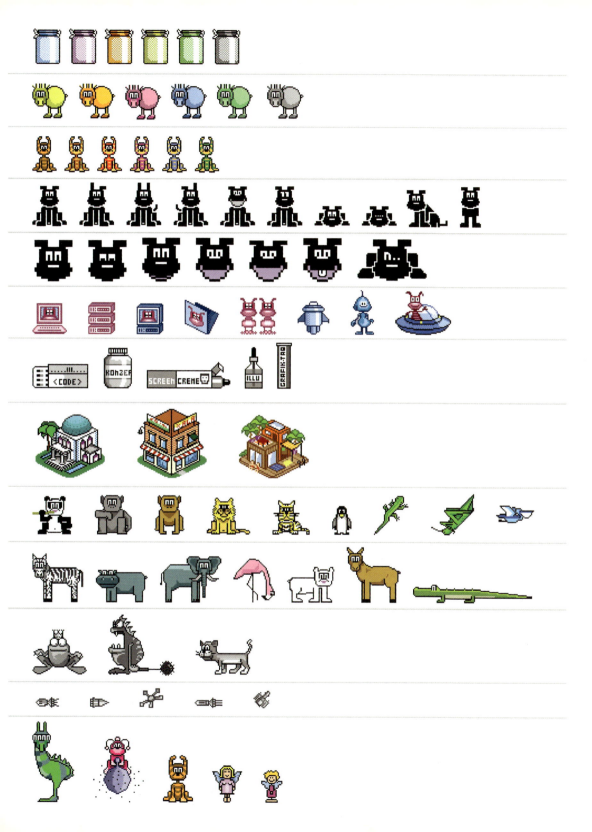

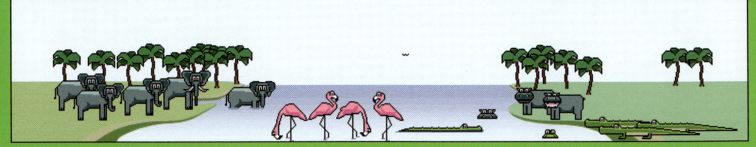

NO.I IN THE 'CUT-OUT AND KEEP' POSTCARD SERIES

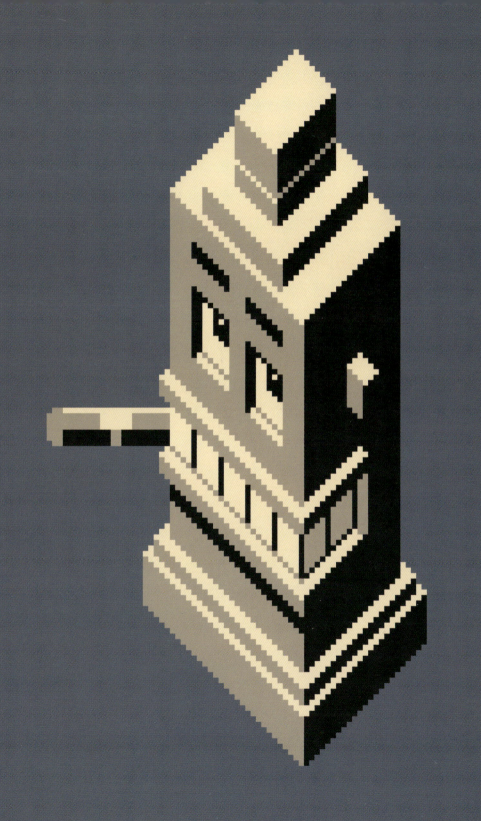

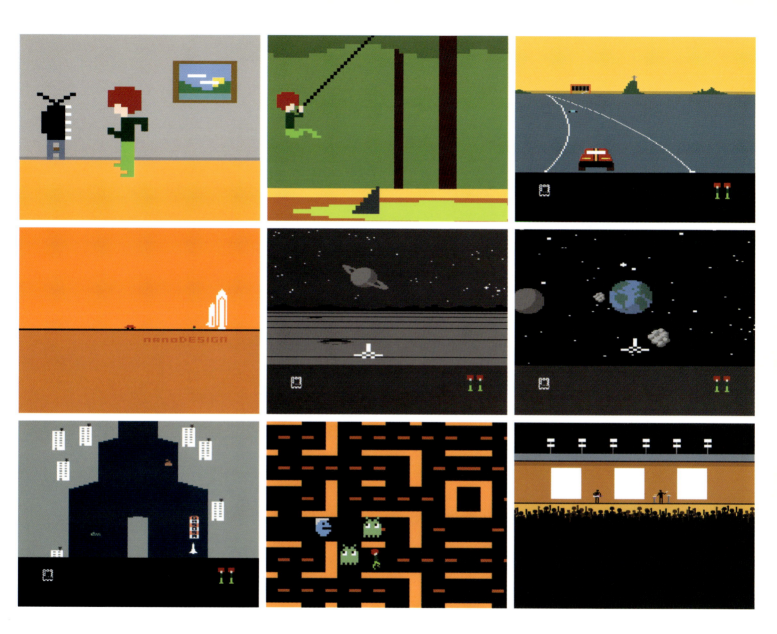

058 ZONK

059 ASP

060 pixelboy

062 ZORA

061 VIOLA

066 drive

065 stars

067 camouflage

063 OTO

064 cross

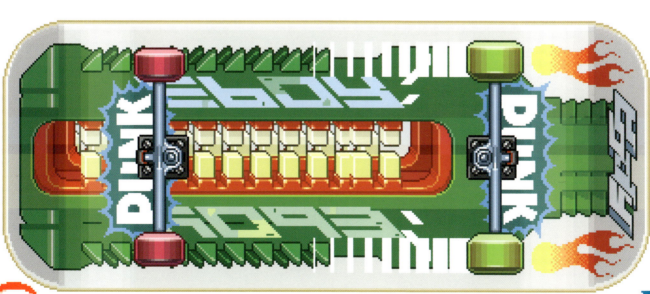

068 FARU

2

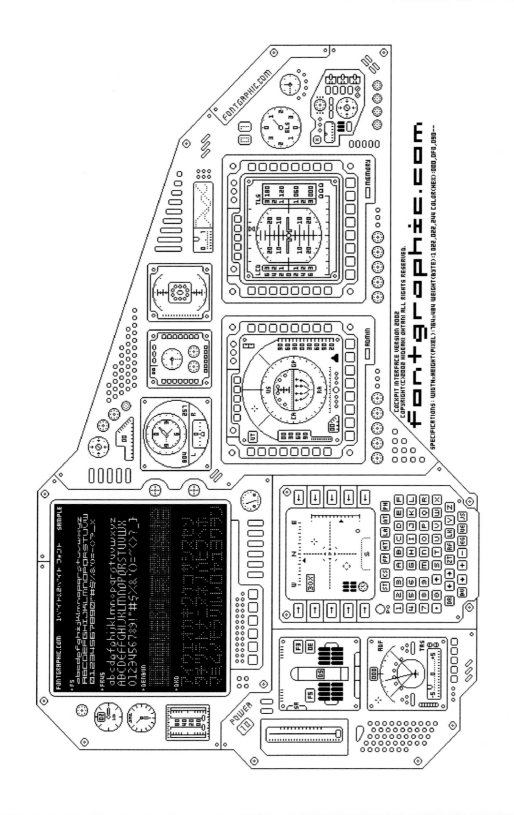

ELECTRONIC AUDIO.MP3

mp3 for u and me   guerrilla audio distribution

音楽 ◨◫◫
download プレセント

1 2 3 4 5 6

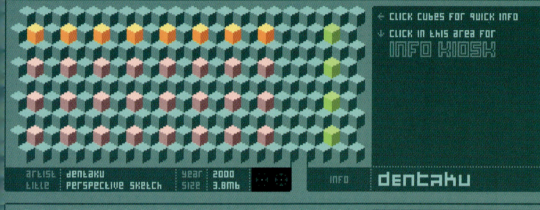

← CLICK CUBES FOR QUICK INFO
↓ CLICK IN THIS AREA FOR
INFO KIOSK

| artist | dentaku | year | 2000 |
| title | perspective sketch | size | 3.8mb |

INFO   **dentaku**

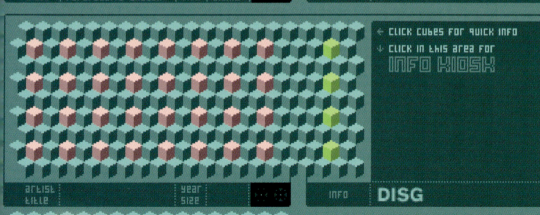

← CLICK CUBES FOR QUICK INFO
↓ CLICK IN THIS AREA FOR
INFO KIOSK

| artist | | year | |
| title | | size | |

INFO   **DISG**

| LINK CHECK | TKAB | EM411 | 2063 MUSIC |

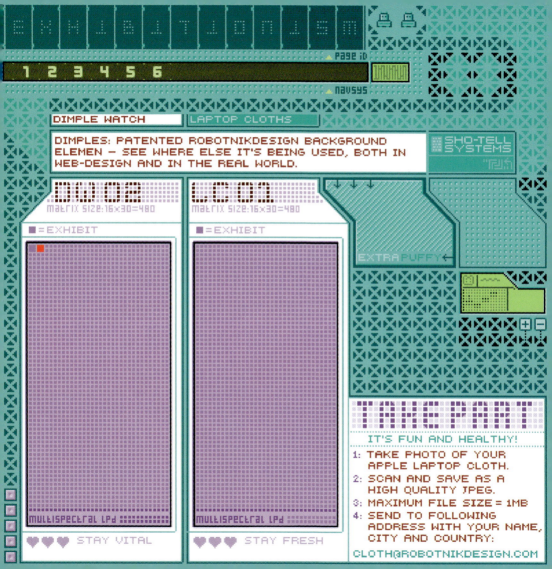

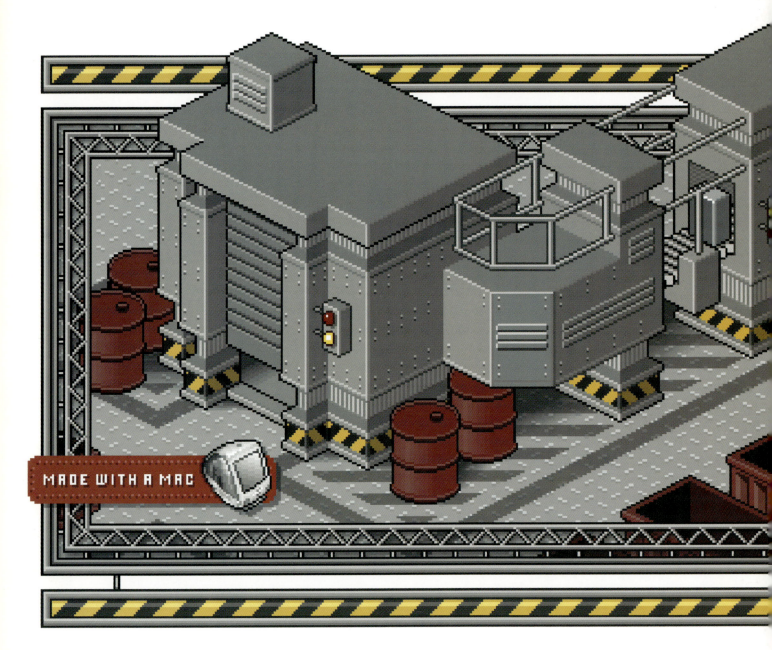

MADE WITH A MAC

See how easy it is!
STEP BY STEP

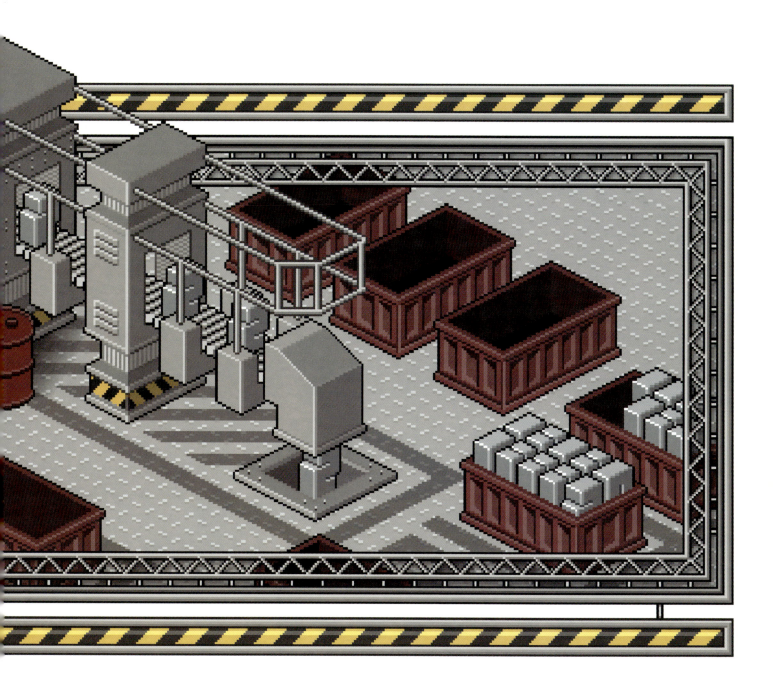

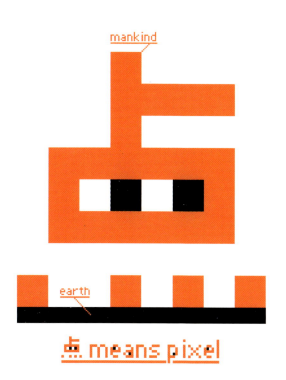

mankind

earth

means pixel

163

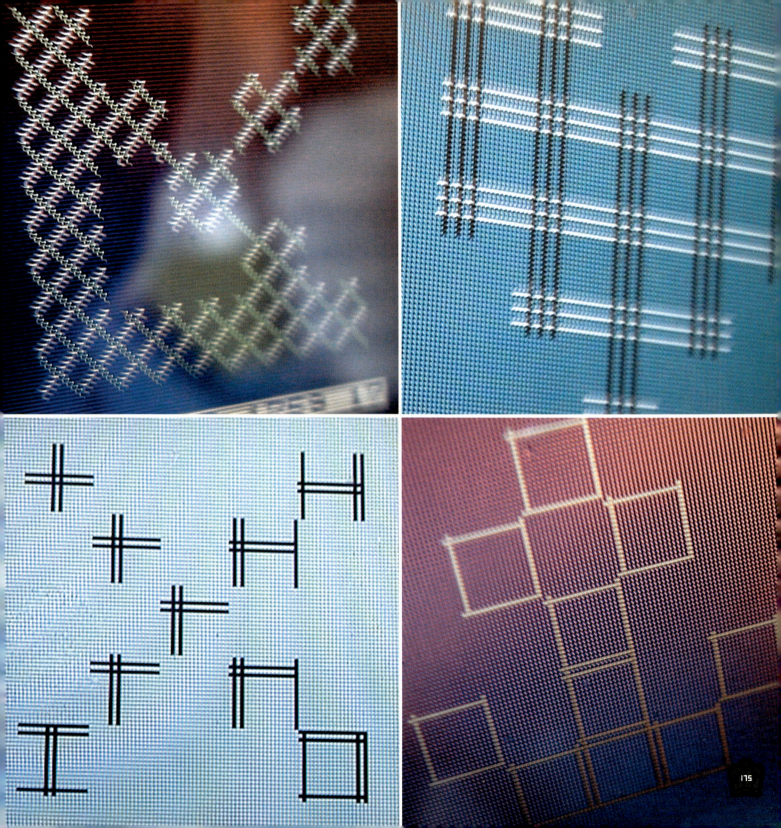

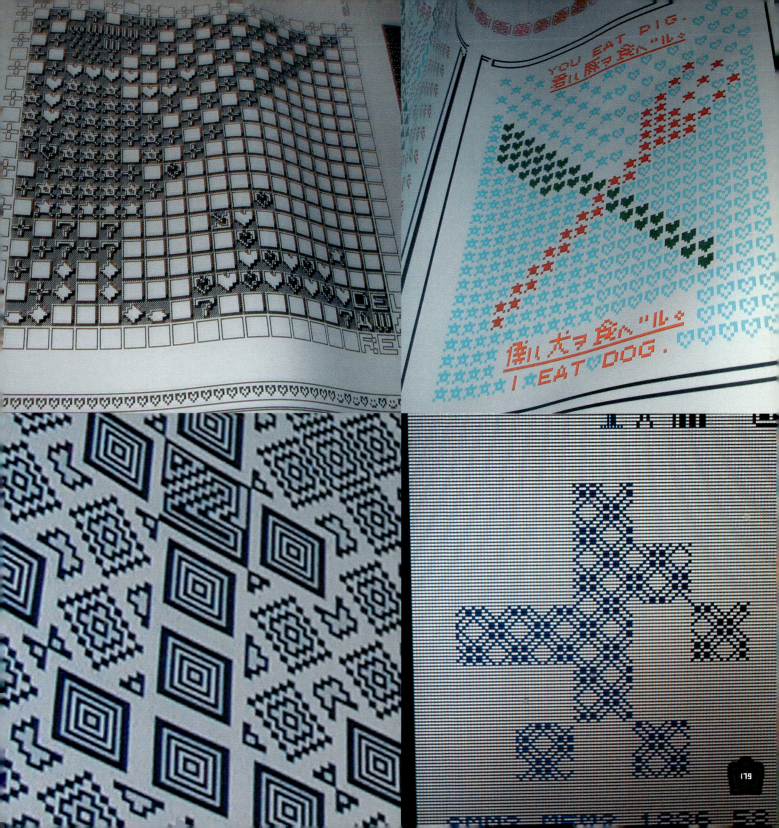

YOU EAT PIG.
君ハ豚ヲ食ベルゝ

僕ハ犬ヲ食ベル・
I EAT DOG.

IN THE MIDDLE OF DIFFICULTY, LIES OPPORTUNITY

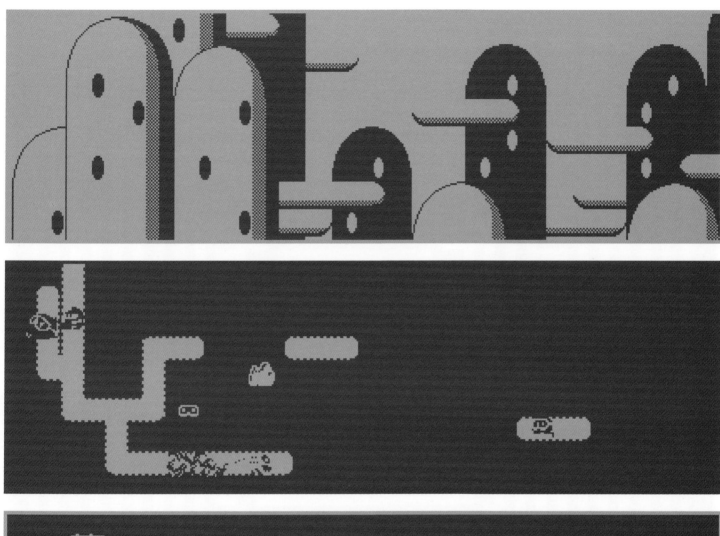
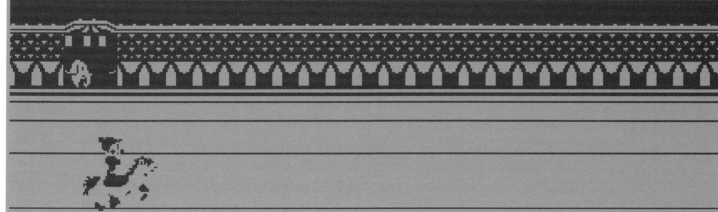

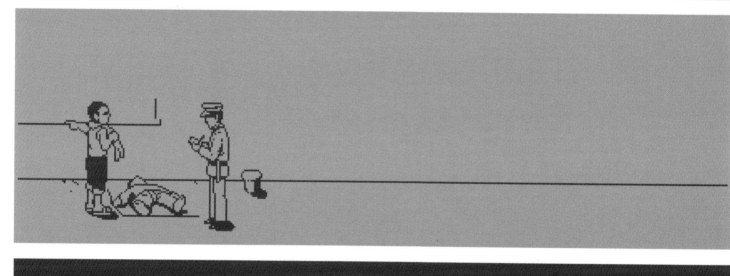

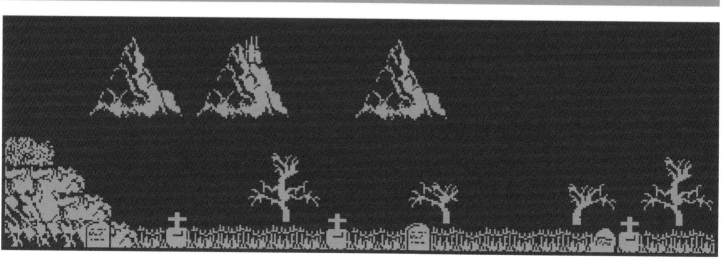

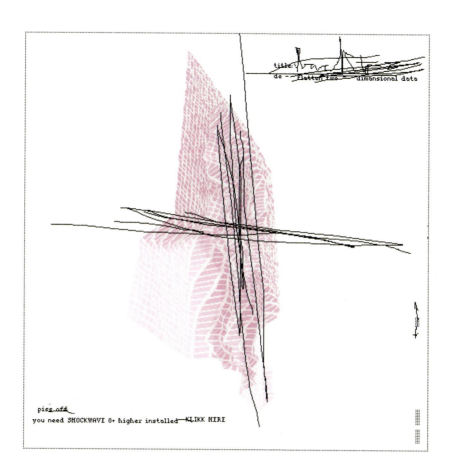

title:
de – flatten two – dimensional data

piss off
you need SHOCKWAVE 8+ higher installed—KLIKK HERE

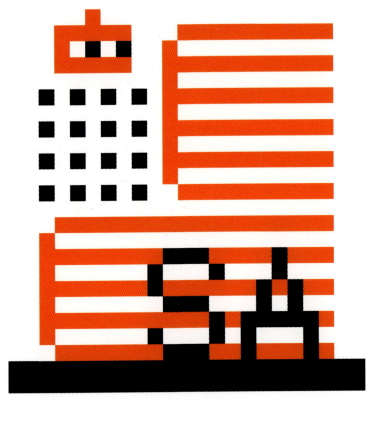

USA

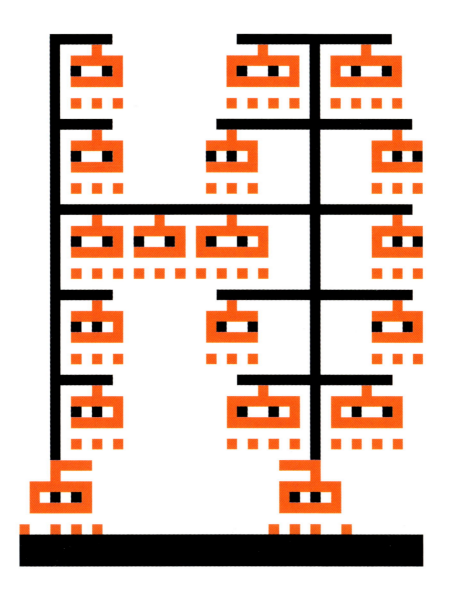

Russian

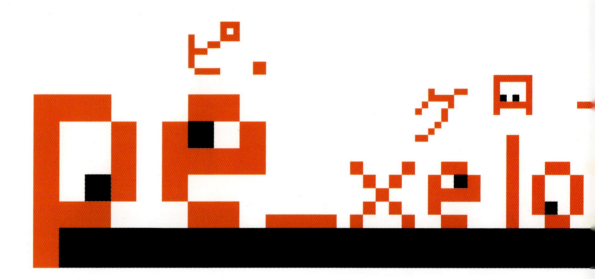

what is gl

パ リ ゼ イ ショ ン ？

alization?

balization?

195

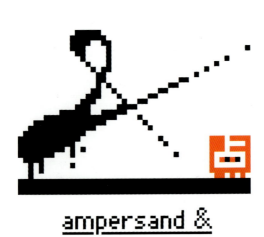

ampersand &

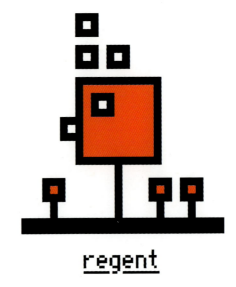

regent

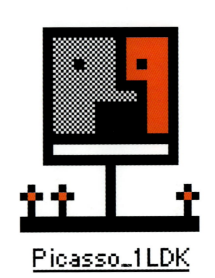

electric elephants

Picasso_1LDK

adam

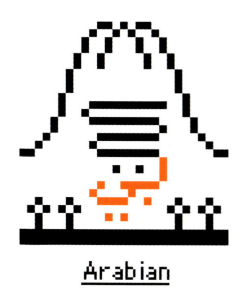

Arabian

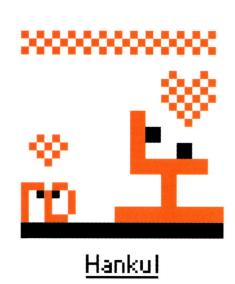

Hankul

philosopher

197

IIIII KU-S

SCORE
00000

HAZRE®

IIIII KU-S

IIIII KU-S

IIIII KU-S

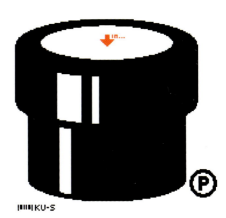

IIIII KU-S

ME OVER

ADISE ?
? ???

IS 19 HILLIO LIGHT YEARS AWAY

IIIII KU-S

VALKYRIE
SCORE   HEALTH
0   750
SELECT HERO

INVISIBLE MONSTERS IN T
ARE LOCATED USING THE RAD

IIIII KU-S

JOYSTICK UP PICKS HEADS
JOYSTICK DOWN PICKS TAILS

IIIII KU-S

PLEASE
INSERT COIN

IIIII KU-S

199

Title:Pad
2002.6.20/180mm×180mm

KU-s

SCORE: 0.69
HIGH SCORE: 0.69
PREVIOUS SCORE:0.00

|||||KU-S

TIME
0.00

|||||KU-S

PLAYER1

|||||KU-S

INSERT
1:30 PER C

|||||KU-S

GAME OVER

|||||KU-S

BREAK
THROUGH

|||||KU-S

CREDIT START >
™

|||||KU-S

TGNG
TOKYO GAMERS NIGHT GROOVE

|||||KU-S

SHOOT
HERE
FOR
PLAY
GAME
®

Title: Game over
2002.6.20/180mm×180mm

200ok
gregor, hnehls
Berlin

gregor / 1967 Born in Regensburg. / 1989 Five years of religious training and studying in the cloisters of the Franciscan brotherhood of Sankt Augustin. / 1996 Started studying visual communication with a focus on digital media at the University of Fine Arts, Berlin. / 1998 Joined the digital-media department.

hnehls / 1975 Born in Hamburg. / 1995 First jobs as graphic-design and aerosol freelancer for ABB, MTU Europe and various public institutions. / 2000 Joined Prof. Joachim Sauter's digital-media department. Studied architecture at the UDK Berlin. Worked for the Fraunhofer Institut, Berlin.

Adept Vormgeving
Joost Van Lierop, Barbarella Haccou
The Netherlands

Adept Vormgeving is a studio for graphic design working with professional software and hardware. We specialise in making house styles, brochures, packaging and other printed media. We also design, build and manage websites.

Ala Webstatt
Switerland

1968 Born in Zurich, Switzerland. / 1993 London. / 1996-1998 Paris. / 1999 Foundation of Ala Webstatt. / 2001 Atelier together with chmork.net.

Arjan Westerdiep
The Netherlands

Master of Arts Image Synthesis & Computer Animation (MA ISCA) at Utrecht School of the Arts (HKU), The Netherlands. Utrecht School of the Arts (HKU), Faculty of Art, Media & Technology, Image and Media Technology, The Netherlands. Graphic School, Eindhoven, The Netherlands.

Brian Taylor
Scotland

Brian Taylor works from home in Dundee, Scotland. He has worked in many areas of design over the years and part-time lecturing at art college. He also pursues his own personal work including his short-film Rustboy and accompanying website rustboy. com, and his portfolio site KL5design.com.

Craig Kroeger
Wisconsin

Craig is a principal of Fourm Design Studio (www.fourm.com), located in Milwaukee, Wisconsin, with fellow principals Jd Hooge, Ty Lettau and Erik Natzke. When Craig is not designing fonts, micro interfaces or unnecessary identities.

Delaware
Japan

Ideal pixelworld of Ala Webstatt

A Japanese super sonic group, designs rock and rocks designs. Works and activities include many things from music CDs and CD-Roms to commercials, magazines, T-shirts, websites, mobile-phones and live shows. Its style, a mixture of music and graphic design, was explored at Mac Expo '98.

Dong Jiangwei
China

"I'm a Chinese pixel artist. The reason why I am contributing is that I want to let more Chinese people know about and love pixel art. Of course, if you want to know more about Chinese pixel art, you can visit my website: ourcall.org."

Eboy
Kai Vermehr, Peter Stemmler, Steffen Sauerteig, Svend Smital
Berlin

Steffen Sauerteig, Svend Smital and Kai Vermehr started Eboy in 1998 – Peter Stemmler from New York joined them some time later. Steffen, Svend and Kai work in two studios in Berlin, Germany, while Peter works in New York.

Francis Lam
Hong Kong

Francis started his own website, db-db.com, as his own design playground. Besides, he is also working on some interactive projects exploring the possibilities of expressing art and technology in the digital media.

Hideaki Ohtani
Japan

Ideal pixelworld of Delaware

Japanese website designer and font creator Hideaki Ohtani works for a Japanese printing company, but promotes his own projects, including his original fonts, on his own websites, www.2x26.com and www.fontgraphic.com, which have both been online for several years now.

Holografix
Isao Yamanaka, Masatake Motoba
Japan

Isao Yamanaka and Masatake Motoba were both born in Osaka in 1972. They studied graphic design in senior high school. Motoba is currently working in the graphic design office while Yamanaka is working freelance.

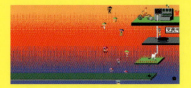

Ian Warner
Berlin

1974 Born in Slough, England, near the Mars factory. / 1993-1996 Study communication design in Portsmouth. / 1999 Version 1.0 of www.robotnikdesign.com goes online. / 2000 Become partner at Grappa Blotto. First project with native instruments as interface designer.

Itai Rabinowitz
Israel

1979 Born in Jerusalem, Israel. / 1998-2001 Graphic designer in I.D.F. service. / 2001-Now Working as a graphic designer.

Jonas Loefgren
Sweden

Currently located in Stockholm, Sweden. Graduate student of Hyper Island School Of New Media Design; recently spent six months at netbabyworld.
www.little-eskimo.com

Kim
Malaysia

My name is Kim, born in Malaysia (1977). I took a diploma course in graphic design in Kuala Lumpur for three years. After school, I began my web-design career in 2000 with a Chinese entertainment website in Malaysia. Then I started to design my first personal website, Redrabit.com, on May 1, 2001.

I ♥ PIXEL!!!

Ideal pixelworld of Holographix

Little Factory
Dennis, Maggie
Hong Kong

Little Factory is a little corner of the web for us to share works and ideas with others. We make icons, wallpaper and all kinds of pixels. We like to get to know different people. We like to work. We don't talk too much, but our door is always open for pixel enthusiasts to join.

Lobo
Brazil

Founded in 1994, Lobo is currently working in association with Vetor Zero to offer solutions in design, animation and content.

Lovepixel
Taiwan

"I was born in Taiwan, and I am 25 years old. Since 1999, I have been making icons of various figures and putting them on my first site for downloading. In the process of icon-figuring, I derived more and more pleasure, and I gradually came to love the kind of art that needs bit-by-bit pixels to contruct."

Meomi
Vicki Wong, Michael Murphy
San Francisco

Meomi is design company co-founded by Michael Murphy and Vicki Wong. Meomi specialises in visual narratives, character design, illustration, animation and motion graphics. It is a strong advocate for pixel critters though it is open to exploring creatures of other materials.

Quickhoney
Nana Rausch
New York

1967 Born in Heidelberg, Germany. Star sign: Leo. / 1989-92 Lette Verein Berlin, school for graphic design, graduated as a designer. / 2000 Founded QuickHoney, together with Peter Stemmler, working for editorial clients such as New York Times Magazine, ESPN, SPIN, VH1 and Fast Company.

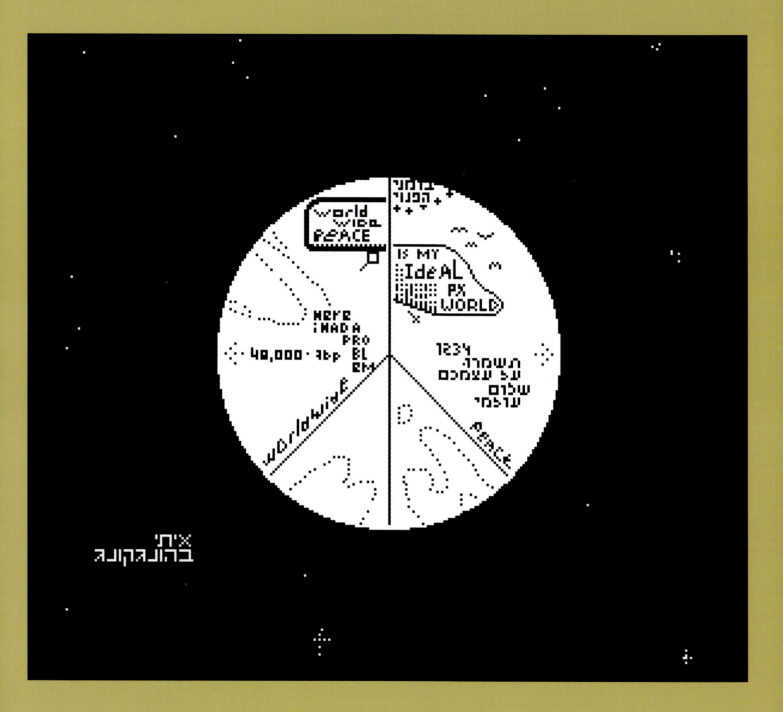

Ideal pixelworld of Itai Rabinowitz

Shinya Inamura
Japan

Education: 2000, Niigata University, faculty of economics. Occupation: web designer, graphic designer, programmer, dot mapper, webmaster of www.everydayicons.jp. Launched www.everydayicons.jp in May, 1998.

Steffen Schaefe
Saxony

The founder of Habitat 7 – a design playground from Germany. www.habitat7.de

Sulake Labs
Finland

Sulake Labs is a private company that creates spatial net evironments utilizing its proprietary technology. The background of the company goes back to the autumn of 1999, when the founders of Sulake Labs, Aapo Kyrölä and Sampo Karjalainen, created Mobiles Disco (www.mobilesdisco.com).

Ten_do
Japan

Ten_do was launched in November, 2001. It participated in a group called Delaware as a guitarist who does not play the guitar, as a lead vocalist, as a graphic designer who "plays" design. It has designed many CDs, CD-Roms, websites, magazines, books, T-shirts and live shows.

USA

Russian

what is globalization?

TGB Design
Japan

Ideal pixelworld of Lovepixel

TGB Design is a unit of Ishiura, Ichifuru and Komiyama. Basically, its members work individually in their favourite fields. They are making CD covers, editorial, websites, advertisements, CF, reflections, CG, CD-Rom titles and so on.

Toshiyuki Iwasaki
Japan

(CD-ROM icons contributor)

"When I was a child, I liked comics and often drew manga. However, my speciality at university was economics. I am working for a clothes-related company now. Therefore, I only make icons as a hobby. I won a contest called "Pixelpalooza 2002"."

Totto Renna
Milan

Totto Renna is a napolitan illustrator and graphic designer who lives and works in Milan since 1990, the year in which he is awarded the diploma in graphics and illustration by the Istituto Europeo di Design. His work can be seen over at: www.supertotto.com

Tsuyoshi Kusano
Japan

In 1999 Tsuyoshi Kusano formed a graphic and editorial unit called LEVEL1 with rolling Uchizawa and Tsuyosh Hirooka. It works for variety of media based on graphic design, including illustration, editorial and motion graphics.

Wig_01
United Kingdom

Wig-01 is a creative partnership dedicated to creating work that doesn't "play safe". It is passionate about creating graphic design – and only works with clients who want to separate themselves from formulaic, mediocre design, and who are prepared to take risks.

Yuji Oshimoto
Japan

Designer based in Tokyo. See: www.04.jp.org

Ideal pixelworld of 200ok

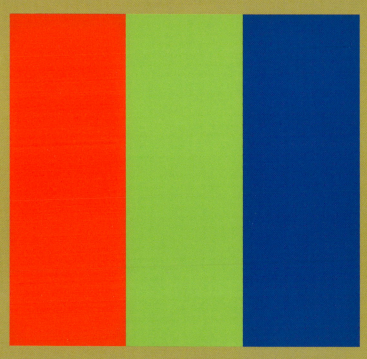

Ideal pixelworld of Wig_01

My ideal Pixel world:

Everything in this world can give me inspirations to do pixel illustration; I wish I can turn everything I see I love to pixel graphic. The world we are living now is my idea pixel world.

Ideal pixelworld of Kim

Ideal pixelworld of Delaware

pixelworld

Co-Published in 2003 by IdNPRO and Laurence King Publishing Ltd

ISBN: 1856693686

Concept: Francis Lam (db-db.com), sk Lam
Editor: Francis Lam
Design: Francis Lam
Book Packaging design: Francis Lam, sk Lam
Production: Chloe Tang
Senior PR executive: Christy Ko
Promotion and Marketing: Portia So, Stephanie Ho

Special thanks: Bryan Leung, Gregor, Hnehls, Joost van Lierop, Barbarella Haccou, Ala Webstatt, Arjan Westerdiep, Brian Taylor, Masashi Ichifuru, Adriano Vannucchi, Mayumi Kaneko, Steffen Sauerteig, Yuji Oshimoto, Nana Rausch, Isao Yamanaka, Masashi Ichifuru, Dennis, Ian Warner, Jonas, Masato Samata, Vicki Wong, Tsuyoshi Kusano, Shinya Inamura, Sampo Karjalainen, ten, Itai Rabinowitz, Tosh, Chosyu, Ilou, Craig Kroeger, Steffen, Andrew Townsend, Matoba Masatake, Angel Chan.

Systems Design Limited
The Publisher of IdNPRO Publications
Shop C, 5-9 Gresson Street
Wan Chai, Hong Kong
Tel: 852 2528 5744
Fax: 852 2529 1296
Email: info@idnworld.com
www.idnworld.com

Laurence King Publishing Ltd
71 Great Russell Street
London WC1B 3BP
Tel: +44 20 7430 8850
Fax: +44 20 7430 8880
Email: enquiries@laurenceking.co.uk
www.laurenceking.co.uk